"One of the greatest discrepancies of our time is between the limitless, God-given resources at the church's disposal and the limited impact they are making on the world. Ronnie Floyd shows that it doesn't have to be this way any longer. We don't have to be a generation of wasted potential. We can turn the world upside down with the gospel. *Our Last Great Hope* shows us how."

Steven Furtick, Lead Pastor, Elevation Church;
Author, *Sun Stand Still*

"In *Our Last Great Hope*, Ronnie calls us to get honest with ourselves about how we are working to help those in desperate need for a Savior. He challenges us to engage the next generation to do the work that Jesus himself called us to do. A must-read."

Greg Surratt, Lead Pastor, Seacoast Church;
Author, *IR-REV-REND*

"Ronnie Floyd's book could revolutionize the way we think about the body of Christ and its purpose. Read it and be inspired, changed, and equipped for our most important mission while on this earth."

Dr. Bruce Wilkinson, Best-selling Author, *The Prayer of Jabez*

"Ronnie's book brings us back to center, crystallizes the pure message of Jesus Christ, and equips the church with how to begin doing these things today. Never before has the church so desperately needed the wisdom and direction offered in these pages. I'll be pulling this book off my shelf again and again!"

Pete Wilson, Author, *Plan B* and *Empty Promises*

"Ronnie Floyd approaches missions-centered living with heart, passion, and inspired strategy. This book is an energizing wake-up call to today's churches, equipping and inspiring us to pursue unreached millions around the world with the saving love of Christ."

Dr. Ed Stetzer, Director, LifeWay Research

"My friend and co-laborer for the gospel, Ronnie Floyd, calls true believers and the church to return to the clear proclamation of the One who is our last great hope, Jesus Christ. His call is passionate—do it now. His message is purposeful—go make disciples. His book is practical—read it and learn. I commend it to you."

Dr. James MacDonald, Senior Pastor, Harvest Bible Chapel

"Ronnie Floyd calls us to an urgent personalization of the Great Commission. *Our Last Great Hope* outlines a strategy and provides practical action points on how to penetrate the lostness of the nations. This book will fan the flames of awakening in your soul."

Dr. Ted Traylor, Pastor, Olive Baptist Church, Pensacola, Florida

"Revival presumes pre-existing life. But so many churches are populated by pre-tenders, assuming they have life when in fact they are spiritually dead. That's why for many years now, I have been urging the true believers of America's churches to pray for another great spiritual awakening. It is out of such awakenings that the course of nations has been radically altered, churches have experienced renewed surrender to the Lordship of Christ, and church members have been catapulted around the globe in answer to the missionary call. In this book, my friend Ronnie Floyd addresses the concept of awakening with his typical intensity and passion, leaving no question as to its necessity. I believe God will use this book to stir the body of Christ to pray for what Floyd calls 'our last great hope.'"

Dr. Tom Elliff, President of the International Mission Board

"Ronnie Floyd has done it again! *Our Last Great Hope* is one of the best, if not the best, training resource to help us move forward with Great Commission fulfillment in our lifetime. You will find the practical insights and powerful principles to be life changing and life saving. Get your copy today!"

Dr. Ben Lerner, Founder, Maximized Living;
New York Times Best-selling Author

"Giving our lives for His cause is His call in the Great Commission. Dr. Floyd passionately challenges and inspires us to embrace His heart for our neighbors and the nations. Read and assimilate this truth and go light your world."

Dr. Johnny M. Hunt, Pastor, FBC Woodstock;
Former President, Southern Baptist Convention

"There's no denying that Ronnie Floyd's life has been changed because of a renewed passion and all-or-nothing commitment to the Great Commission. Pick up this book and you can't help but be pulled in by his excitement. Ronnie challenges us to ask, do we really love Christ passionately, and if we do, are we willing to do whatever it takes to follow through on His Great Commission challenge? Ronnie challenges us to see that if we are to seriously embrace that charge it will mean dramatic change in our personal lives, our families, our churches, and our finances. This book asks a lot—nothing less than a sold-out heart and life. But it's just what Christians and the church need if we are to share with the world *Our Last Great Hope*."

Dr. Kevin Ezell, President, North American Mission Board

"In his final words on earth, Jesus challenged every Christian to reach the world with His message. We call it the Great Commission. Yet, too often, we allow the monotony of life to distract and dissuade us from experiencing the power found in those words.

"In *Our Last Great Hope*, Dr. Ronnie Floyd pushes us past predictability and points us to a deep, intimate knowledge of why we are here. He shows us what it takes to carry out the Great Commission in today's world. And he empowers us with tangible ways to discover the promise, purpose, and passion of Jesus' words."

Ed Young, Pastor, Fellowship Church;

Author, *Outrageous, Contagious Joy*

"Ronnie Floyd inspires me to trust our risen Lord to do extraordinary things through my most ordinary life and my most mediocre moments. The transparency found in Pastor Floyd's words are both convicting and convincing. The time for change is now. *Our Last Great Hope* should be your first required read."

Dr. Leonard Sweet, Best-selling Author of *Jesus Manifesto* and the Soon-to-be Released *I Am A Follower: The Way, Truth and Life of Following Jesus.*

"Never has the hour been more urgent for people to respond to the good news of Jesus Christ. I know no pastor with a greater burden for the lostness of our world than Ronnie Floyd. His book is a great challenge and inspiration for us all."

Dr. Bryant Wright, Senior Pastor,

Johnson Ferry Baptist Church, Marietta, Georgia;

President, Southern Baptist Convention

"Frequently a long pastorate grows stale. Not so with Dr. Ronnie Floyd, who has led his church to do precisely what he writes about here: namely, to undertake the task of getting the gospel to the whole world in every conceivable way. This is not a book of theory. This is a book about what has happened in Northwest Arkansas. Its message will encourage every pastor!"

Dr. Paige Patterson, Southwestern Baptist Theological Seminary,

Fort Worth, Texas

"We have heard about, preached about, talked about, and taught about the Great Commission . . . but how many of us are consumed by it and truly know the magnitude of what it entails? I know of no one with a passion for Christ, His Word, and His church like Ronnie Floyd. He has beaten out every one of the principles in this book on the anvil of his own personal experience. Read it and you too will be convinced it is . . . *Our Last Great Hope!*"

Dr. O. S. Hawkins, President and Chief Executive Officer,

GuideStone Financial Resources of the Southern Baptist Convention

"Ronnie Floyd is one of the greatest leaders of our day! He has given his life and ministry to the Great Commission of our Lord. His latest work is an urgent call for Christians, churches, and denominations to make a new commitment to an old commission. Warning: this book will change lives, communities, and the world!"

Dr. Grant Ethridge, Senior Pastor, Liberty Baptist Church;
President, Southern Baptist Convention Pastors' Conference 2012

"Ronnie Floyd is giving the church a book on the Great Commission that pastors and church members can read and personalize. He also shares practical things a church, a family, and an individual can do daily and weekly that allow them to be a part of the Great Commission."

Bob Roberts, Senior Pastor, NorthWood Church;
Author, *Real-Time Connections* and *Global Engager*

"*Our Last Great Hope* is an inspiring, engaging, visionary, and informative work from the pastoral and missional heart of Ronnie Floyd. I pray that this book will be used of God to strengthen Christ-followers and church leaders for the lofty and demanding call that has been given to the churches in this global and challenging context of the twenty-first century."

Dr. David S. Dockery, President, Union University

"We have an *emergency* due to a lack of *urgency*. With souls in the balance and millions who have yet to hear the gospel, *Our Last Great Hope* calls every believer to the forefront of fulfilling the Great Commission. Dr. Ronnie Floyd passionately calls upon every Christian to get to the front lines of sharing the message of Jesus to a lost and dying world."

Dudley Rutherford, Pastor of Shepherd of the Hills Church,
Porter Ranch, California

"In *Our Last Great Hope,* pastor Ronnie Floyd challenges those who follow King Jesus to personally own the Great Commission, to come to a place where we find it inconceivable to leave the work to others. Every church should be a Great Commission church. Every Christian should be a Great Commission Christian. This book will help its readers see how."

Dr. Daniel L. Akin, President, Southeastern Baptist Theological Seminary

"The Christian's Mount Everest is the fulfillment of the Great Commission. No previous generation has ever placed the cross of Christ on the roof of the world. Dr. Ronnie Floyd's remarkable book, *Our Last Great Hope*, causes us to get real about the enormous size of this global mountain and creates Christ-centered hope of scaling it in our lifetime! Once you have read this profound resource, you will view your remaining moments and years as currency either spent on endless trash or invested into eternal treasure. Read it now and reap forever!"

Dr. James O. Davis, Cofounder, Billion Soul Network, Orlando, Florida

"Ronnie Floyd does not spin theories or weave conjectures; he challenges, convicts, and calls the church to a deeper commitment to reach the world for Jesus Christ. What Ronnie Floyd writes, he not only believes . . . he lives out."

Dr. Mac Brunson, Senior Pastor, First Baptist Church, Jacksonville, Florida

"Ronnie Floyd is a straight shooter with the ability to both encourage and challenge. That's what you will find in these pages—the encouragement that the Lord is at work through us and the challenge that we need to say yes to everything He calls us to do. Read this book to sharpen your heart and move toward becoming the Great Commission believer Christ desires!"

Gregg Matte, Pastor, Houston's First Baptist Church;
Author, *Finding God's Will*

"*Our Last Great Hope* is a sterling reminder that the Great Commission has not been rescinded. Ronnie Floyd has given the body of Christ a treatise on why we must put the 'go' back into the gospel. As I read this book, I once again became keenly aware that evangelism is not an optional plan of the local church; it is an essential priority."

Dr. Stan Toler, General Superintendent, Church of the Nazarene,
Oklahoma City, Oklahoma; Best-selling Author

"Pastors everywhere are looking for more time and energy to fulfill the will of God for their lives. *Our Last Great Hope*, written by Ronnie Floyd, helps us to peel away the nonessentials in our lives and to double our efforts to finish Christ's goal for the earth. This remarkable resource is the ticket to a faith-filled journey of Christ-centered living for Great Commission fulfillment!"

Dr. Timothy Hill, First Assistant, Church of God, Cleveland, Tennessee

"Finally there is a powerful life-giving book to equip Christians from all walks of life. *Our Last Great Hope*, written by Ronnie Floyd, is destined to become one of the greatest books for pastors in particular and Christians everywhere. If you lost a sense of divine destiny or truly want to invest the rest of your life, this powerful resource will impact you now, tomorrow, and forever."

Dr. Ademola Ishola, General Secretary, Nigerian Baptist Convention,
Lagos, Nigeria

"Heaven is for real, and with that thought, Ronnie Floyd calls every Christian to reach the lost in *Our Last Great Hope*. The Great Commission was not just a suggestion but a command to every Christian to share the news of Jesus Christ."

Dr. Fred Luter, Senior Pastor, Franklin Avenue Baptist Church,
New Orleans, Louisiana; Vice President, Southern Baptist Convention

"I have devoted my whole life to networking in the body of Christ for the fulfillment of the Great Commission. Ronnie Floyd, in *Our Last Great Hope*, helps us to get on the same page, with straightforward steps to becoming a part of something bigger than ourselves—namely the fulfillment of the Great Commission. This is a turnaround book, where ordinary people are equipped enough to turn their lives around before it is too late. Your life will be enriched forever!"

Dr. John Ed Mathison, President, John Ed Mathison Leadership Institute; Pastor Emeritus, Frazer Memorial United Methodist, Montgomery, Alabama

"This is a marvelous read! My good friend Ronnie Floyd has touched God, and through his words he touches us so that as we read we in turn can touch others."

Dr. Elmer Towns, Cofounder, Liberty University, Lynchburg, Virginia

"I am thrilled to recommend *Our Last Great Hope* to pastors and their local churches, along with Christian leaders worldwide. This single powerful resource will teach you how to bring eternity home to your family and your church. You will find your heart renewed and revived for the things that matter most and less interested in the nonessentials of the Christ-centered life. Read it today!"

Rev. Casey Treat, Christian Faith Center, Seattle, Washington

"I determined years ago that I would do my best to train everyone possible in Great Commission principles for the multiplication of the global church. In *Our Last Great Hope*, Ronnie Floyd challenges us to move from competing with each other to completing together the Great Commission as soon as possible. It could become one of the quintessential books for this generation!"

Dr. David Sobrepena, Founding Pastor, Word of Hope, Manila, Philippines

"*Our Last Great Hope* is more than a book; it is the personal guide to helping to fulfill the Great Commission and being prepared to give account of our lives before the Lord in eternity. When you have read the words of Ronnie Floyd, you will find you have more time to do what really matters in this life and less time to waste for the temporary things that are passing. This volume reminds us that the Great Commission is not an option to be chosen or ignored by the believer but is a divine commandment that affects eternity. Read it and reap from it!"

Dr. Douglas LeRoy, General Director, Church of God World Missions, Cleveland, Tennessee

"Every Christian needs a Christ-centered compass, and every church needs to be equipped to reach its maximum potential. *Our Last Great Hope* by Ronnie Floyd will compel you to higher levels of personal spiritual development, while at the same time outlining a biblically based path to truly helping the entire world to know the gospel before it is eternally too late."

Rev. Paul Louis Cole, President, Christian Men's Network Worldwide, Fort Worth, Texas

"I believe both young and seasoned Christians should make *Our Last Great Hope* an annual read, just to stay with the kingdom-minded agenda of doing all we can to fulfill the Great Commission as fast as possible. Ronnie Floyd writes from his personal experiences and demonstrates the changes necessary to stay on course. Be sure to get a copy for yourself and for your friends!"

Dr. Prince Guneratnam, General Superintendent-Emeritus, Assemblies of God of Malaysia; Senior Pastor, Calvary Church, Kuala Lumpur, Malaysia

"God is raising pastors and planters worldwide. *Our Last Great Hope is* a priceless resource that pastors and their respective churches must have throughout the earth. I am thrilled there is a cutting-edge resource that communicates to all ages of society through both biblical and practical means for physical and spiritual victory. Ronnie Floyd is to be commended for bringing this kingdom-minded book to the body of Christ worldwide."

Rev. Suliasi Kurulo, Founding Pastor, World Harvest Centre, Suva, Fiji

"Ronnie Floyd will expand your personal and professional vision in *Our Last Great Hope*. He champions a global mandate to work together to finish the Great Commission in our lifetime. If you wish to move the insignificant to the magnificent, then read *Our Last Great Hope* today!"

Rev. Eddy Leo, Founder, Abba Love Ministries, Jakarta, Indonesia

"Ronnie Floyd has brought to the global church *Our Last Great Hope* in a time when we need to be reminded that our role is to fulfill Christ's goal. This eternal goal is wrapped up in the Great Commission. Pastor Floyd carefully unpacks his personal journey and shows us how we can truly help to make it harder for a person to live on this planet and not hear the glorious gospel of Christ. This valuable resource is destined to raise the leadership level in the church worldwide."

Dr. David Mohan, General Superintendent, Assemblies of God, Madras, India

"Ronnie Floyd will stretch your thinking like never before in *Our Last Great Hope*. I cannot stress enough the importance of you reading and applying the godly teachings found within its pages. You will be motivated, for the rest of your life, to keep the main thing the main thing until everyone has heard the eternal gospel of Christ."

Rev. Leon Fontaine, Founding Pastor, Springs Church, Winnipeg, Canada

"*Our Last Great Hope* will make you dissatisfied with living the rest of your life without taking the gospel to unreached people groups throughout the world. Our goal is to plant more than 200,000 more churches in East Africa in our lifetime, and I believe *Our Last Great Hope* will inspire and instruct our leaders to do so!"

Dr. Alex Mitala, New Birth Fellowship, Kampala, Uganda

"Very few leaders have the visionary ability to communicate in such terms to stretch us in new frontiers of personal leadership development. Ronnie Floyd, in *Our Last Great Hope*, moves from the reached to the unreached regions of the globe. He sets the visionary standard for every local church and shows the path to truly helping to fulfill the Great Commission in every world region."

Dr. Gustavo Crocker, Church of the Nazarene Eurasia Director, Switzerland

"Ronnie Floyd gets it. He's captured the need and the opportunity before us. Taking the gospel to the world is not optional. It's not an item in a buffet line that you can pass up. It's part of God's menu for His followers. As you feed your soul on these pages, you'll find a balanced blend of Scripture, personal stories, and historical accounts. This book made me hungry to do more to reach my community and the world."

Dr. Michael Catt, Senior Pastor, Sherwood Baptist Church, Albany, Georgia; Executive Producer, Sherwood Pictures

"Over the last two decades, I have come to know Ronnie Floyd as one of the most mission-driven pastors serving the church today. He is an amazing leader with a heart for missions and evangelism and a rare ability to mobilize Christians to take action in obedience to Christ. It has been a joy to work alongside him, and it is with eagerness that I recommend this book."

R. Albert Mohler, Jr., President, Southern Baptist Theological Seminary

"Ronnie Floyd has the voice of a prophet, the heart of a pastor, and the spirit of a disciple-maker. This book awakens a slumbering church from apathy, anarchy, and apostasy to fulfill an assignment given by our Lord to a people who have Hope for a world who desperately needs it. Warning: When you wake up, don't hit the snooze button."

Ken Whitten, Senior Pastor, Idlewild Baptist Church, Lutz, Florida

Our Last Great Hope

AWAKENING THE GREAT COMMISSION

RONNIE FLOYD

THOMAS NELSON
Since 1798

NASHVILLE   DALLAS   MEXICO CITY   RIO DE JANEIRO

Published in Nashville, Tennessee, by Thomas Nelson. Thomas Nelson is a trademark of Thomas Nelson, Inc.

Thomas Nelson, Inc., titles may be purchased in bulk for educational, business, fund-raising, or sales promotional use. For information, please e-mail SpecialMarkets@ ThomasNelson.com.

Unless otherwise noted, Scripture quotations are taken from HOLMAN CHRISTIAN STANDARD BIBLE. © 1999, 2000, 2002, 2003 by Broadman and Holman Publishers. All rights reserved.

Scripture quotations marked ESV are from THE ENGLISH STANDARD VERSION. © 2001 by Crossway Bibles, a division of Good News Publishers.

Library of Congress Cataloging-in-Publication Data

Floyd, Ronnie W., 1955–
  Our last great hope : awakening the great commission / Ronnie Floyd.
     p. cm.
  Includes bibliographical references (pp. 223–226).
  ISBN 978-0-8499-4707-0 (trade paper)
  1. Great Commission (Bible) 2. Evangelistic work. 3. Missions. I. Title.
  BV2074.F56 2011
  269'.2--dc23

                                                            2011024374

Printed in the United States of America

11 12 13 14 15 QG 5 4 3 2 1

I dedicate this book to my very special friend
Johnelle Hunt, and to her late husband, J. B. Hunt.
I loved J. B. dearly:
as a teacher of lessons of life and leadership,
as one who found joy in seeing others come to Christ,
and as the model of a servant devoted
to the global advancement
of the gospel.
Jeana and I cherish Johnelle:
a gracious and loving woman
and a wonderful, giving friend.
Individually, these two are God's best;
together, they have built one of the
great companies of North America—
yet more than this, they have laid at God's feet
the resources He entrusted to them,
for the reconciliation of their world
through the fulfillment of the Great Commission.
May the favor of God shine richly
upon the legacy of
J. B. and Johnelle Hunt.

Contents

CONTENTS

CONTENTS

Overflowing with Gratitude

I was delighted when Thomas Nelson Publishers approached me about writing a book on the Great Commission of Jesus Christ. I said a prayer of thanks to God, for I recognized His hand yet again.

Great Commission strategizing ignites my spirit like nothing else. I long to exhaust all approaches, and all resources, in telling every person in the world about Jesus Christ and making disciples of all the nations. This has been my heart for many years. But now, after a life-changing period of deeper focus on the task, the time was absolutely ripe. My passion for such a project was at high tide.

But what kind of a book? Nelson wanted one not about theory but about *action*. Those were just the words I longed to hear, for this is the essential moment for action. That Nelson would choose me for this subject was humbling; but it was their vision for an *urgent* and *practical* book that won me over.

These, I recognized, were people who had been listening to God. They understood the work His Spirit was bringing to a boil during our time. They embraced the vast undertaking—humanly impossible, divinely inevitable—of finishing the work that Jesus mandated for us twenty long centuries ago.

Therefore, I must begin by expressing my heartfelt gratitude to my Lord and the corporate servant He has in Thomas Nelson.

As God did with Paul, so He still does: that is, advance the gospel person to person, through a chain of loving relationships. Thomas Nelson's Jack Countryman and I have been friends for years. I believe that friendship has culminated in our partnership in this work.

Under God's leadership, Jack shared with Matt Baugher what he sensed God wanted to do. In a short amount of time, Thomas Nelson presented me this opportunity formally.

With a passion to get this book out, Matt called his gifted team to join us by ensuring this project is executed. Therefore, I am so grateful to God for Matt Baugher, Jack Countryman, Jennifer McNeil, Emily Sweeney, Stephanie Newton, and the entire team at Thomas Nelson.

My relationship with them led me to receive assistance in this project from Rob Suggs, a gifted writer and wordsmith. I am so blessed and overwhelmed with gratitude for having Rob alongside me for this moment.

There is no way I could avoid mentioning the experience that changed me forever. Johnny Hunt, then president of our convention, appointed me to serve as chairman of the Great Commission Resurgence Task Force of the Southern Baptist Convention. I led a team of twenty-two diverse leaders in bringing a report and recommendations to our convention of more than forty thousand churches and congregations, on the question of how we might better work together to fulfill the Great Commission.

Besides pastoring Cross Church, I led this gifted team for

one year through, long, exhausting and exhilarating hours. Therefore, I am overwhelmed with gratitude for these friends who joined me in this one-year journey: Danny Akin, Tom Biles, John Cope, David S. Dockery, John Drummond, Donna Gaines, Al Gilbert, Larry Grays, J. D. Greear, Ruben Hernandez, Harry Lewis, Kathy Litton, Albert Mohler Jr., Mike Orr, Frank Page, Jim Richards, Roger Spradlin, Ted Traylor, Simon Tsoi, Robert "Bob" White, Ken Whitten, and of course, Johnny Hunt. Thanks for investing in my life and in this Great Commission journey.

Behind the scenes in this Great Commission journey was a gifted group of people who were intricate to helping us accomplish our work. My heart is overflowing for the service and work of Kim Whedbee, Anita Stewart, Kathy McClure, Andy Wilson, Jim Law, Mike Daniels, and Nick Floyd.

I am also thankful for the International Mission Board and North American Mission Board for their contribution to the vast majority of statistics shared through this book. Their research departments, who work with other researchers globally, are so very skilled at assisting churches.

Last but not least, I am also grateful for my wife, Jeana, who has been my partner in life for thirty-five years. These past two years, she has sacrificed our time together to get us to the point of releasing this book. In the first year, she had a husband that had two full-time jobs. In the second year, she has encouraged me to embrace this project and write it with conviction and heart.

Therefore, to Jesus Christ, to all of these, and to you, I am overflowing with gratitude.

One thousand thank-yous,
Ronnie W. Floyd

Encounter on a Mountaintop

Not far from the summit, Matthew paused to catch his breath. The morning sun was insistent, and the climb was tiring.

"Not much farther," said John with a smile, seeing his friend's weariness. John was a younger man with a smaller frame. He loped uphill without breaking a sweat.

"I just hope we're right about this," said Matthew. "How do we really know?"

"He'll be here," said John firmly. "I feel it. And I think some of these others do too."

It was strange. Just like the old days, the crowds were converging on the path—scores of people. Yet they were quiet, most of them, wrapped in their thoughts, in their hopes of an encounter at the mountaintop. Maybe, like John, they could feel Him moving somewhere inside themselves.

Matthew wasn't sure what he felt, other than uncertainty about the future. Once he had collected the taxes. It was a nice living, if an unpopular one. It was over now; he couldn't go back to working for the Romans, not after these three years. He was no longer that Matthew. These fishermen—Peter and the others— could ease into their old lives as they would a familiar old cloak. Matthew's life was an open question. He glanced at this little group, now eleven with the defection of Judas. Together they'd slipped out of the city and into Galilee a few days earlier. There was safety here, but more important, the Master's promise that He would be present. At the time they'd hardly listened. He'd spoken many times of crosses and tombs, but who could believe it? Surely it was some kind of parable, some dramatic hyperbole.

But Jerusalem had been no parable. Its events were a confusing tangle in Matthew's mind now, a fever dream he could not interpret. He remembered the usual chaos of the Passover, the streets clogged with the masses: impatient centurions, shoving and cursing; vendors hawking; drunks and beggars wailing; religious leaders lurking wherever the Master walked. He remembered a quiet Passover dinner Thursday night. It was a holy dinner: the Master nearly whispering, some air of sad finality in His manner, the air in the room heavy like at a funeral. He remembered the garden, dozing off, and then . . .

Daybreak. Peter and James shouting, everyone in chaos. *Taken!* They're holding Him! On the streets, some were saying the high priest had Him; no, said others, it was the Romans who bore Him away. The Master was accused of sedition—plotting to destroy the temple.

He was gone. The eleven of them were now orphans—no direction, no plan—lost in an endless day of fear. "They'll come for the rest of us!" All of them were lying low, the women weeping and baking bread, the men bickering. Then His mother and

John had come in, pale, despondent, telling it—the worst, the unthinkable. He couldn't be dead.

But he was. Nailed up like a criminal. Wrapped up quickly, sealed away without so much as a full burial. The end. The new life, the Way, the hope—all of it was over. The Romans were still in power; the people of God were still in humiliation. Nothing had changed. Matthew's anger had contended with his grief. He recalled it now to his shame. *Fools, all of them!* he had thought. Three years, for this. And then . . .

Sunday morning.

The women—not the eleven—the women were the ones to see Him! Matthew remembered scoffing at them, at their insistence He was not dead. Women's hysteria. And yet . . . *Oh, if it could be true!* He had promised it, had He not? But how in heaven?

Peter and John bolted toward the tomb while the others sat simply dumbstruck, and now the rumors were flying:

He is risen. He is risen!

Even the Romans got involved, claiming the body was stolen (as if that were possible). The two men from Emmaus were absolutely certain they had walked the road in His company. Ten of them—all but Thomas—talking, arguing about it on the following Sunday, and then . . .

The Master Himself, standing among them, as if it were simply another day, as if the nightmare had never come. Standing there, like a dream, but changed somehow. The deep cuts in His wrists and His feet. And His laughter! Laughter that could scatter demons.

Everyone was weeping, kneeling. Worshipping.

The memories all ran together in Matthew's mind as he trudged up the hill. He had been there. There wasn't enough imagination in a tax collector to conjure such a vision. The Rabbi had been dead but was not dead. It was a wonder beyond comprehension: He was alive again, but not in the same way; not among them, not a traveling companion. Indeed He had come to Galilee, some of them said. Seven of them had seen Him on the beach, even had breakfast with Him. The first sighting outside Jerusalem. All of them understood that a new day had dawned, but what kind of day?

Matthew lifted his eyes as they came to the top. People were milling around or sitting and resting, looking everywhere. He closed his eyes for a second, a prayer asserting itself from the pit of his stomach, and when he opened them, he was looking into the face of Jesus.

It was the Master, some ways off, beneath the branches of a tree. He was calm, contemplative. As He was spotted, voices and questions were raised. Some weren't certain. But the disciples knew, and again they found themselves prostrate, praising and exalting their risen teacher and friend and Lord. So many questions, so much they all wanted to tell Him.

Jesus began to walk toward them, and he gently shook His head; He had one more lesson to teach. Matthew and the others then sat down all around Him, knowing this time that each word must be captured, remembered. Someday perhaps Matthew would preserve the story in writing.

Jesus said, "All authority has been given to Me in heaven and on earth." He paused a moment as they let the words permeate their minds. He had made such statements before; now it was so much easier to believe.

He continued, "Go, therefore, and make disciples of all nations, baptizing them in the name of the Father and of the Son and of the Holy Spirit."

It was a startling command. Matthew had listened to the Romans talk about their travels. The world was a large place. Some said it stretched beyond the known seas, beyond the mountain barriers, to strange lands even Caesar didn't know. "Make disciples—of all nations." Matthew scanned the faces of the disciples, and of all the others present, trying to visualize the words of the Master.

"Teach them to observe everything I have commanded you," Jesus said. "And remember, I am with you always, to the end of the age."

Matthew had his future now. Unlike anything before, it was a task bigger than him, and there would be days when it would seem futile, like attempting to capture the sky in a little cistern. But he had His promise too: "I am with you, always." Those words held power. They held promise.

. . .

Tradition holds that Matthew died as a martyr in Ethiopia, one of those distant lands, some sixty years later. Like most of his friends, he exchanged his life for obedience to the commission he had been given. Almost all died in far-flung nations: in India, in Greece, in Judea, in Phrygia, in Italy, in Persia, even in Britain. By the time the last of the eleven, John, died, there were new disciples of Jesus Christ in every corner of the Roman Empire and beyond it.

By the fourth century, that empire was in its death throes, yet people all across it worshipped Jesus. Then Western civilization fell into a long sleep, as did the church. Even after ten centuries of cultural darkness gave way to a new awakening, the Christian faith in many ways continued its slumber. The command to make disciples of all nations was preserved in the written testimony of Matthew, studied by monks, and eventually bound and printed by Gutenberg's new printing press. But few obeyed it.

There were no organized missions anywhere on the globe until 1783, when a British Christian named William Carey began to read of Captain Cook's exploratory voyages to Australia and other places. He looked at a world map, and he thought about the many countries where people had yet to hear the news of Jesus Christ, almost eighteen centuries after the Lord had been taken up into the clouds. His heart began to burn with the desire to go and make disciples of those people.

By this time, Carey was pastor of a small Baptist church. At a gathering of ministers, he raised the question, wasn't it the duty of all Christians to do as Jesus had commanded them? Carey was told that Jesus had been speaking only to the disciples then living. It applied only to the first century, and the charge was no longer binding. Appalled, Carey decided he would work by himself if he had to. He wrote a pamphlet setting out his plans to take the gospel to every nation, beginning with India. Even his best friends told him England had plenty of work for him to do without worrying about other countries.

Eventually Carey left for India with no funding whatsoever, just his own determination. He faced years of hardships, the mental illness of his wife, the death of a son, nonstop criticism from home, and, most disheartening, very few converts. "Yet this is our encouragement," he wrote in his journal. "The power of God is sufficient to accomplish everything that he has promised, and his promises are exceedingly great respecting the conversion of the Heathens."[1] He would one day coin the phrase, "Expect great things from God. Attempt great things for God."

About the same time, over in the young United States of America, a revival known as the Great Awakening was sweeping the countryside. William Carey's pamphlet came into the hands of a convert named Samuel Mills. During a thunderstorm, he and several college friends took refuge under a haystack, where they found themselves praying about taking the gospel to every nation. Soon they were organizing their own missions society, and the idea caught fire. In time, the modern missionary movement arose from their initial work as various denominations, and religious groups began organizing missions to many countries. The gospel began once again, after many quiet centuries, to move into new lands. Leaders began to speak of the Great Commission.

Still most of God's children slept on. They worried about the daily concerns of their lives, the issues of their communities, and perhaps the questions of their faith. Few were those who burned with passion to do what Jesus had instructed, to "make disciples of all nations." Missionaries seemed like odd, eccentric characters rather than champions of the faith. The church slumbered on until the world, like the Roman Empire two millennia before, began to show signs of coming apart, until even those with little interest in religion began to wonder if the end was near.

Then God placed in certain hearts a new awareness of the Great Commission. Suddenly people of God began to step forward, their hearts burning to see global evangelism, worldwide discipleship, and the Spirit of God being poured out upon the whole world. A younger generation was less nationalistic and more compassionate toward other cultures. New mission strategies began to materialize, but the work seemed harder than ever before. Some asked, "How can it be done?"

A few voices in the crowd responded, "With God, there will be a way. All things are possible through Christ. Besides, we have no choice—this, the fulfillment of the Great Commission, is our last great hope."

CHAPTER 1

Face the Truth About Yourself

Imagine a group of important leaders calling you into a fancy boardroom. They say, "Okay, we've selected you to be in charge of changing the world forever. Your job is to create a delivery system that will reach every single person in the world. Oh, and it needs to be done *yesterday*."

Actually, something like that happened to me.

I was humbled, to put it mildly, on the day I received the challenge. I was asked to serve as chairman of the Great Commission Resurgence Task Force of the Southern Baptist Convention. Sure, it sounds like just another church committee. Bureaucratic titles make even the miraculous sound mundane. But there's nothing dull at all about this endeavor—not when you really think about it, not when you truly understand what's at stake on Planet Earth. And I did understand—or at least I thought I did, in the beginning. I knew all about the Great

Commission. When Jesus ascended to heaven, He left us with a mandate to penetrate every corner of our world with His message, His offer of salvation from the sin that destroys us. His charge went like this:

> Go, therefore, and make disciples of all nations, baptizing them in the name of the Father and of the Son and of the Holy Spirit, teaching them to observe everything I have commanded you. And remember, I am with you always, to the end of the age. (Matthew 28:19–20)

The Great Commission had already been my passion; it's the lifeblood of my denomination and of evangelical Christianity. So you can imagine the fire that was lit in my soul when I was asked to chair such a group. The task force involved twenty-two leaders and thinkers with a mandate to study for one year and then bring forward fresh insights about what might be the most effective way we could finally do what we haven't done in two thousand years—penetrate the unreached world with the gospel and make disciples of all the nations. I knew this was the most wonderful, significant opportunity I would ever undertake in my earthly life.

Upon further review, however, I began to feel overwhelmed. I only thought I knew what it meant to fulfill the Great Commission. It's a stated goal that Christian groups throw around almost casually. We voice it all the time, because it's what we all want to do. Now, however, I realized the magnitude of the quest. It was like hearing about the Grand Canyon all your life, maybe seeing a few pictures of it, and then actually standing there at the edge of it for the first time, with the wind whipping at your collar and a great, fiery sunset on the western horizon. There's just no way to be prepared for the awe and wonder. The reality outstrips the simple concept. The Great Commission really is a simple concept:

Tell every person in the world about Jesus Christ and make disciples of all nations.

That's a mission statement so basic a young child can grasp it. But the reality of the Great Commission—well, that's another story, and I had not come to terms with it.

Our task force read widely. We studied. We investigated. As a result, we came to grips with a vast, sprawling, complex, rapidly changing global village. We considered the languages, the cultures, the new opportunities and ancient obstacles of communicating our message to seven billion people, each soul as unique as his or her fingerprints, each one infinitely precious to God. In this "Grand Canyon moment," we were overwhelmed by reality, and we knew we had to be honest with ourselves. We weren't playing games.

Defining the task accurately would be mind-bending. And that was just for starters. We would also have to convince sixteen million Southern Baptists in over forty-five thousand churches that our definition was the right one, and that this endeavor should become the great work of their lives. We would be responsible for making everyone see the reality of this work, while remaining excited about forging ahead with it ourselves. Now do you begin to see why the idea of awakening the Great Commission is staggering?

Jesus said to us in Acts 1:8, in the other great statement of the Commission, "You will be My witnesses in Jerusalem, in all Judea and Samaria, and to the ends of the earth."

He was talking about a ripple effect, ever-expanding circles of massive salvation, each one a new and different demographic reality. Jesus intends us to answer, what is the reality of Jerusalem? of Judea? of Samaria? of your neighborhood, your gender, your generation, your socioeconomic group? Those who came directly after Him—the generation of the apostle Paul—made those ripples happen in spectacular fashion. The first Christians moved across languages and cultures, defying hostility, languages, demonic opposition, and tremendous odds, until our faith won out over the greatest political empire in history, the Roman Empire. The gospel was shared; disciples were made in many nations of that period.

So we know it can be done, and we have at our disposal all kinds of technology and tools that Paul and his fellow missionaries didn't have. But consider the obstacles, even for those who embrace the challenge of defining reality. That technology is a two-edged sword. We live in a world of misinformation. Media reporters and political leaders throw out new falsehoods every day so that we fail to understand our world and even ourselves. A barrage of TV commercials push us toward the belief that personal happiness is tied up in how many toys we own or in how many varieties of physical pleasure we pursue. The opinion makers—their reality has changed too. Their legions have swelled exponentially in our generation through technology, particularly the Internet. Our eyes and ears and minds are constantly filled with the white noise of this blog or that talk show—and so few of those are bound up in the truth we know to be in God's eternal Word. So many opinions, so much advice, yet there is one God and one truth. In the incessant babble of our times, I'm driven to God, to hear the only voice that matters.

I hope your head isn't already spinning. When we discuss awakening the giant, mobilizing the Great Commission for this world at this time, we must start somewhere, and that means, of course, at the most basic level: ourselves. We can't define the reality outside us until we handle what is within. I must therefore begin with myself—and with my God.

A High-Def Mirror

The first battle to be fought is the one for my heart and soul. I know my limitations. I look inside, see how fallen and helpless I am, and know my only hope is to trust Him. There is a wonderful passage in the New Testament that cuts to the heart of this problem of the inconsistencies in my spiritual life:

> But be doers of the word and not hearers only, deceiving yourselves. Because if anyone is a hearer of the word and not a doer, he is like a man looking at his own face in a mirror; for he looks at himself, goes away, and right away forgets what kind of man he was. (James 1:22–24)

In this word picture, the man looks into a clear mirror. Mirrors don't lie; they define reality in full color. Let's imagine this man sees a dab of toothpaste stuck to his chin. It makes good sense for him to wipe off the smudge, right? Someone who is not a doer of the Word, James tells us, is like a man just leaving the paste there. He is ignoring the truth that has just been presented to him.

God's Word is a mirror that shows us who we are in high definition. It defines reality with harsh precision. As I read the Bible, I find that this book has me nailed. What all those political leaders, Madison Avenue wizards, and Internet chatterers—even my closest friends—don't understand about me, the Scriptures do. I open the covers, gaze into the reflection, and see myself looking back. The reality of myself. This is why we are disciplined to study our Bibles every morning to prepare for the day spiritually, just as we look into the bathroom mirror to prepare for the day physically.

Reading the Word, I'm humbled. I'm encouraged. I'm strengthened because I know exactly where I stand. But when I finish my morning devotional time, put aside the Bible, and get busy with my day, I'm in danger of losing the reality I've been shown. I need a disciplined mind and will; I must cling to the truth as I begin to walk through this world, knowing that thousands of competing messages—sometimes subtle, always powerful, generally lies—will assault my thinking. If Scripture is a high-definition mirror, then these are fun-house mirrors. They seek to amuse us by telling us agreeable lies about ourselves.

I must admit that I am the source of my share of these competing messages. I am tempted to rationalize my sin, to play games rather than be honest, or to take the easy way out during those defining moments of life, when it's absolutely critical that I know how to be honest with myself. Whether it's some disembodied voice in technology or some inner voice generated by my foolish pride or spiritual laziness, I must ignore the world's lies and follow the Word's truth. Narrow is that path, Jesus tells us, the path of self-honesty; wide is the avenue that leads to destruction (Matthew 7:13–14).

I also need to be aware of my concern for image and perception. Just like you, I want to be loved, accepted, and admired; it's a matter of human nature. But we can become slaves to the approval of others. We want to please other people at all times. For the best and most valid of reasons, we want to please a spouse, a supervisor at work, a leader at church. We want our friends to think highly of us. There's nothing wrong with any of that—until approval becomes our defining reality. Then our quest for approval becomes a lifelong pursuit of fool's gold.

Life is to be lived for an audience of One. Here's an encouraging thought: if I can focus utterly and completely on pleasing God, suddenly life becomes very simple. I've defined my path, and His Word will light that path for every step. I no longer need to listen to all the competing voices out there. I may not please all the people all the time, but I will do my best to live as God wants me to, and that will be my reality. Ultimately we must all make that choice, as Paul did: "For am I now trying to win the favor of people, or God? Or am I striving to please people? If I were still trying to please people, I would not be a slave of Christ" (Galatians 1:10).

It's time for me to get real—to be honest with myself and before God. Do I want the truth? Can I handle the truth?

Our Last Great Hope

Why all this talk about reality and honesty? I raise these questions for one reason. Take a good look around you, at the direction of our world. All things considered, would you say it's a better or a worse place than a few years ago? Set the parameters of your evaluation any way you choose: our nation, the international scene, popular culture, our economy, our ecology, our politics, our families. Most of us would answer that we are a generation in decline. Many Christians believe that Christ may return soon. Even nonbelievers sense that calamity awaits us in some form.

If we, with all our technology, all our intelligence, and all our human philosophies, had the solution to this decline, don't you think we would have produced it by now, in these thousands of years of human civilization? Modernism hasn't created utopia. Science has created as many problems as it has solved. I must conclude that our last great hope lies beyond our human capabilities. The course of civilization has borne out what the Bible has said all along: we are fallen and deceived creatures; whatever we try—by our means—will be doomed to corruption because we are innately corrupted by our own sin.

There is one last great hope—for our world, our nation, our children, and our churches. That hope only becomes visible when we become honest, when we define reality rightly. That hope lies in the person and power of Jesus Christ and in no one else, in no other path or possibility. We call it good news, even though there is nothing new about it, because every new moment, every new problem, every new sin, has already been conquered and forgiven through His suffering and death on our behalf and His resurrection from the dead on that Easter morning two thousand years ago. There is good news for whatever is ailing in your life; good news for whatever challenges confront you tomorrow and next week; good news for every single conceivable human problem we face today. But it is good news that must be delivered and then accepted.

Years after the Second World War was over, there were Japanese soldiers still holed up on the Pacific Islands. No one had gotten them the news of surrender. They could have gone home to be with their families, but the good news had not been delivered. As a matter of fact, when the last aging soldier was finally brought the news, he refused to accept it. He convinced himself that it was only an enemy ploy to make him put down his weapons. Only when his commanding officer was personally brought to the island did the old soldier acknowledge that there was peace and that he no longer had to live in caves or fear the enemy.

Our God came Himself to deliver our good news, to tell us that the war between heaven and humanity was over and that both sides won. He put on flesh and walked among us and then, before He left, instructed us to keep on bringing that news. The war is over, but the fighting continues in places where the amazing news hasn't penetrated. Isn't that a tragedy? That's why our task is urgent—Satan is racking up victories in a conflict he has already lost. The head of the serpent has been cut off, and the body is writhing in its death pangs.

The gospel of Jesus Christ is the last great hope for this world. According to the promise of Jesus, we have been given His power, His presence, and His authority—all we need for success. And the Great Commission is our marching order, the operation on which everything depends. It's time for us to awaken to the urgency, the reality, the simplicity of this one task, an assignment beside which all others pale into insignificant trivia.

Think of the ways we allot our time and energy—our causes, our quests, our dreams, our hobbies, and our pursuits. How much eternal importance is in each one? Are we, like the legendary emperor Nero, fiddling while Rome burns? Jesus told us to seek His kingdom and His righteousness first, and all the other things will follow in their proper place (Matthew 6:33). First? I wonder how many of us are even seeking His kingdom second or third or tenth. How many people do we encounter every day who are dying of thirst for the living water only Christ can provide, but we're too busy to tell them?

Someday I will stand before my Father to account for my actions in this life. Oh, how I long to be able to say, "My Lord and my God, I know You gave me Your greatest gift, so I gave all that I could of my time and resources to do what would please You. In my generation, we fulfilled the Great Commission! We finally enabled every living soul on our planet to hear the message You longed to give them, and we made disciples of every nation."

And it is my deepest prayer that I can hear Him say, "Well done, good and faithful servant" (Matthew 25:21, 23 ESV).

A Great Awakening

During these last months, I've felt something change within me, something powerful stirring my soul. I've developed a deep hunger to be about my Father's business of pursuing this mission to our whole world, of carrying out the Great Commission. It's not as if I haven't always been devoted to the task. I've always seen it as the focal point of my personal ministry and all Christian ministry. That passion has been there for me. But lately, that passion has matured. It has taken hold of me from the inside, made me eager, and distracted me from little things that used to seem so important. It's as if all the chaos and clamor of my life have suddenly fallen into place and become one cohesive picture: the image of the Great Commission relentlessly pursued to fruition. I still care about leading my family, leading my church, serving my local community, and all the rest. But these are now like rivulets that lead into the great, raging river that is my charge to take the gospel to the world and see massive, global revival as a result.

What would this world be like if suddenly there was a worldwide harvest? I fall asleep thinking about it, and I wake up with a refreshed vision. In my mind's eye, I see it all as I begin my day—and then I deal with the mundane responsibilities life requires of me. If only I could spend all my time, all my abilities, all my strength on what really matters. I look around and see our streets teeming with people who are consumed by football or politics or Hollywood or Wall Street or the dating scene or the Internet. I understand the lure of all these things. But as for me, I want to trade in my remaining years, months, days, and minutes—God alone knows their count—for the kind of seeds that will take root among people and then blossom in heaven. I now see my moments as currency, and I can spend them on trash or treasure. I don't want to give any precious resource of this life to that which isn't eternally significant.

For me, that means a laser focus on the Great Commission. I hope you might come to feel the same way. Toward that end, we must learn to define reality, to be honest with ourselves. This book is intended to help you do that. The following principle should help you start down that road.

The Waterline Principle

I don't believe I ended up living in Northwest Arkansas by some random occurrence. When God hands out careers and directs the courses of lives, He is purposeful. In my little corner of the world, there are giants in the land—corporate giants, and three of them. Walmart, J. B. Hunt, and Tyson Foods all have their headquarters in the vicinity. One of those is the world's largest business; another is the largest transportation logistics company of its type in North America; the third is the world's largest poultry and beef producer. Walmart alone is a business magnet, attracting more than twelve hundred other vendors to our region. Most of these national and international companies sell and service their products to Walmart.

Did God have a purpose in placing me in this particular commercial hub? I think He wanted to develop in me a great burden for the businesses of the world, and that's what has happened. A decade ago, when our church was launching a new campus in nearby Pinnacle Hills, I began the Summit Business Persons' Luncheon. We didn't design it as a Bible study, but as a vehicle to minister to the needs of corporate leaders. From the beginning those who came to us tended to be members of the wider community rather than simply our church. We focused on equipping people to do business in the right way. At first I was the regular speaker, but over the years we've begun to bring in guest leaders of all kinds.

While that ministry has taken on a life of its own, and I may speak there no more than three or four times per year, I've grown too. I find myself reading important books and magazines from the business world, keeping abreast of that culture. I look for new ways to invest in our Summit leaders as well as the many corporate people in our church. The intricacy of corporate culture is one of those things they don't teach you in seminary; God has built into me a great interest in business, which in turn is one of the keys to awakening the Great Commission—because the business of America, the last great empire, is business.

A couple of years ago, I came across a particularly intriguing book: Jim Collins's *How the Mighty Fall: And Why Some Companies Never Give In*. The author really hits the target, illuminating truths that apply not just to businesses but everywhere—including churches, ministries, and denominations. Collins writes about taking risks "below the waterline." He asks us to imagine being the captain of a ship. Make one bad decision, and you'll blow a hole in the side. If that hole is above the waterline, you have the chance to patch up the hole, learn your lesson, and sail on. But if that hole is below the waterline, you're in big trouble. Water gushes in upon you, and you have to both stop the flood and somehow patch the hole, or you will very soon find yourself on the ocean floor. Great companies, Collins says, don't take risks below the waterline.[1] They know exactly where the impact of a poor decision will be, and they protect what is essential for keeping their heads above water even in risk. I read that passage and underlined it furiously. This writer was talking about defining our reality.

I've counseled people many times and have seen them take terrible risks with their families, their careers, their very souls.

Collins has described what I tried to do—help people see just what would happen if they found the water suddenly rushing in. The problem comes when people won't be honest with themselves. They won't admit exactly where the waterline is. If a man has an affair, that's a below-the-waterline decision for his wife and his children. It will sink the family quickly, no matter how he tries to patch things up later. If a young lady falls in love with a man who doesn't share her faith, she thinks she is well above the waterline, but the opposite is true. If a businessman cashes in his financial reserves to start a business of his own, he'd better have a rock-solid assurance his business will succeed, because those reserves are the waterline for taking care of his family.

What could be more critical to life than simple self-honesty? It's as vital as it is difficult. So how can you make good, above-the-waterline decisions as you define your personal reality?

Three Tough Questions

Being honest with ourselves begins with a willingness to ask the tough questions so we have the opportunity to provide the tough answers. Let's consider some of the questions each of us must ask.

Do I Know Jesus Intimately?

Consider Paul's challenge to the believers in Corinth:

Test yourselves [to see] if you are in the faith. Examine yourselves. Or do you not recognize for yourselves that Jesus Christ is in you?—unless you fail the test. (2 Corinthians 13:5)

Paul was responding to a group of complainers who were questioning his credentials as an apostle. He urged them to be honest with themselves; to step back, look within, and see if there was any sign of Jesus inside. Jesus, of course, would have no part in bickering about Paul's background, or starting church quarrels. Once He has a solid grip on our minds and wills, there is no time for petty squabbles.

Paul's test is still valid. When was the last time you took it? This is serious business because your ultimate waterline is your eternal condition. You wouldn't gamble with your soul, would you? Would you really place your eternal destination at risk? The day will come when it's too late to patch that hole, so you'd better know where you stand.

If you know much about the Christian faith, you'll understand that by virtue of being human, you begin this voyage with a gaping opening in your hull. It can't be repaired by any amount of churchgoing, financial giving, or community service. All of those things are rewarding, but they're only the fruit of a grateful, Spirit-led life. In themselves, they can never wipe away the sin and rebellion in your life. No, we are born with leaky hulls, and the breach grows larger every day. We desperately try to mend them with many other things. But we look closer and see that the hole is in the shape of a cross.

Only Christ, crucified as payment for our sins, can fill the gap. When you realize that, you are ready to bow at the feet of the crucified Jesus and accept the gift He has offered you—the gift of healing, the gift of peace right now, and the gift of a perfect eternal life when this earthly one is over. Once He has fixed that gaping fracture, it stays fixed. Nothing in heaven or earth can sink the ship. It will sail you to a new life and a heavenly destiny.

I'm sure you realize that many, many more people identify with Christianity than actually follow Christ. People go to church for a lot of reasons. For some of us, the reason is that Christ is everything to us. Knowing and serving Him make life worth living, and we are dead serious about being closer to Jesus tomorrow than we are today. But I'm sure you know people, as I do, for whom the adjective *Christian* is just another designation, such as *brown-haired*, *left-handed*, or *American*. Being a Christian is one more identifying trait in a crowded life.

Look again at the question I've posed—Do I know Jesus intimately?—and think about how you would honestly answer it. Take your time—you'll never answer a more important question.

You see, we're talking about the Great Commission. How can someone have a passion for obeying it if he or she hasn't fully internalized its message? What if I asked you to tell people all over town about a new restaurant when you had never dined there? You wouldn't be so excited about that subject, and frankly, you wouldn't be a very effective spokesperson. But if you had been there, enjoyed the specialty of the house, and knew it was the greatest meal of your life—so fantastic you would never want to dine anywhere else, for any meal—then no one could stop you from telling your friends about that place.

If you've truly tasted of the Bread of Life, if you've sipped from living waters that well up to eternal joy, there is absolutely no way you can live without telling others about it. You want everyone to have a chance to sit at that table, even people you don't know—people across the country or across the world. That's why the Great Commission is my passion, and why it should be yours.

Do I Love Jesus Passionately?

I was a college student when I met Jeana, the woman who became my wife. It didn't take long for me to be drawn to her powerfully. I fell head over heels in love, and I organized my life around that relationship. I rearranged my schedule, cut out lesser things in order to spend more time with the woman I loved, and sat up nights figuring out ways to show her how much I cared. No doubt about it: I was *passionate*.

Maybe you've been there. There's something incredibly wonderful about having your life become a nonstop honeymoon. And of course, like most other couples, we progressed to new stages of our relationship. We didn't fall out of love; we didn't start taking each other for granted. But no one can stay giddy and love-struck forever—nothing would ever get done in the world! Maybe we don't offer as many silly, Hallmark gestures of our affection as two nineteen-year-olds might do, but we do enjoy a deeper, fuller partnership in our marriage. We know each other's thoughts, finish each other's sentences, and complement each other with the gifts we each have. That's a pretty wonderful thing too. But our relationship is not all business as usual; it would be sad if we let that happen. Whenever we get the chance, we take off on trips together to rekindle our romance. We work to stoke the passion between us.

Romance and spiritual devotion are different varieties of love, but there are strong similarities between them. Jesus underlined this concept in the book of Revelation, when He was speaking to the church in Ephesus. He began by commending the Ephesians. He told them there were many things they were doing right, but an essential ingredient was missing: "I have this against you: you have abandoned the love [you had] at first" (Revelation 2:4).

He is talking about the love those believers had for Him. Somehow, amid all the great works and ministries the Ephesians were performing, they had lost their passion for the One they were serving. They had created a busy church, but one that lacked its first love of Christ.

The good news, He told them, was that what they had lost could still be found. "Remember then how far you have fallen; repent, and do the works you did at first" (Revelation 2:5).

That verse offers a three-step plan to falling in love with Christ again:

1. *Remember.* He tells them to measure the depth between where they are now in their love and where they once were, to take take a trip down memory lane and feel what has been lost.
2. *Repent.* Neglecting Christ is, to put it simply, sin. Renounce it; make a fresh start. Commit to remain close to Christ and to let nothing get in the way.
3. *Repeat* the things you used to do. In a marriage, this would mean getting back to the time you spent together. It would mean talking more, listening more. With Christ, it's much the same. Start spending more time in prayer, in study of His Word, and in serving others in His name, as perhaps you once did.

Remember. Repent. Repeat. Sounds like a plan, doesn't it? It's a path of restoration to the Christ-centered life. If you do those things, you'll find yourself rediscovering your passion for the Lord, who has such a passion for you. Jesus didn't offer this to the Ephesians as a viable option among many. He told them that if they fail to love Him as they were created to do, then He will judge them for it. A deep love for Christ isn't just a good idea— it's the only thing that makes life work.

I can tell you from my own life that it's all too easy to lose that early passion for Christ. As a new Christian, I couldn't get enough of the Lord. I was constantly found in prayer and regularly immersed in the Scriptures, soaking them up for all they were worth. I was powerfully drawn to the church, where I could be with His other children and we could minister to one another. At some point along the way, however, it all became habit—something I did in the same way I'd shower or brush my teeth. There were times when I had an elevated passion for things that matter to God—say, speaking out against cultural and national sin, or pursuing spiritual programs and movements. But I didn't realize the difference between devotion to His work and devotion to *Him*.

It's a massive difference, that of love versus legalism. I cared about building a growing church, and that was something He wanted. But first He wanted *me*. I cared about mission work, and so does He—but His mission to *me* is the starting point from which all my service must be launched.

I've often had an "Ephesus moment" and realized how far I had fallen. Then, under the loving, comforting guidance of the Holy Spirit—He is never an accuser, but always a loving agent of restoration—I have repented and returned to the things that deepened our relationship. To love Christ passionately is to love Him uniquely, to hold Him above everyone and everything else. It is to grow more like Him every day, so that His values become my values. That means beginning to love people the way I see Jesus love them in the Gospels—humbly, sacrificially, and all-inclusively, so that it's possible to care for people on the other side of the world. Loving Christ passionately is a point from which all roads lead to the Great Commission.

Our last great hope is to rekindle a fully inflamed passion for Jesus Christ, leading to a renewed, all-hands-on-deck urgency to reach His world.

Do I Share Jesus Constantly?

The Great Commission is ultimately a Grave Commitment. It recognizes that our world is in peril, with people perishing every day without a saving knowledge of Jesus Christ. We commit our lives to rescuing as many as we can, as quickly as we can, wherever we can.

We've been thinking about knowing and loving Christ. Now, as we raise the subject of sharing Him, we realize that we can't separate any one of these pursuits from the other two. To know Christ is to love Him; to love Him is to share Him. We want everyone to experience what we have experienced. We want it because we are obedient, because it's natural to share what is wonderful with others, and because those others face an alternative that is terrible beyond imagining.

Authentic faith, then, doesn't come in various sizes. It can't be customized to our preferences. To know Jesus—to really know Jesus and not just to play the game—is to know Him ever more intimately, to love Him ever more deeply, and to follow Him to the ends of the earth and the ends of our lives in obedience to His message. You can't be "sort of" Christian any more than you can be "sort of" pregnant. Once you set out to follow someone, you go where he goes. You walk at his speed.

We look around and realize just how much the world needs this message. It is our task to go to our neighborhood, our region, our nation, and our world in the pattern Jesus set out for us in Acts 1:8. When I listen to Christians speak as if this is the work of "specialists" called missionaries, my heart aches. When someone says, "Don't we have plenty of needs to meet close to home, before we start talking about some country overseas?" I shake my head in sadness, realizing these people have somehow missed the heart of the gospel. Is breathing a task we leave to special people? Is eating? Sharing the gospel globally is as central to our discipleship identity as breathing is to our human identity.

This is another tough truth, and it must be faced. The Christian who is apathetic about the Great Commission is the one who is not walking at Jesus' speed, who has fallen far behind, or who is wandering somewhere in the woods. But if Christ is our guide, the Great Commission is our compass. To know Him is to love Him, to feel an increasing desire to please Him, and finally to realize what it is that He wants from us more than anything else: to share Him with His lost children.

I study the history of Christianity and find one story after another in which this has happened. The young believer starts out simply loving the Lord, and this love inevitably leads the believer to say, "What do you want me to do, O God?" And God's answer is always the same: *Go—find them and bring them to Me! They're lost, they're dying of their hurts, and they need Me just as you do.* For two thousand years, truly godly men and women have stepped forward, been honest with themselves, and come to the conclusion that what God wanted was for them to take the gospel everywhere and to make disciples.

But you say your burden is for your own neck of the woods? That's a start; it could be that you have a special calling to your community. But keep this in mind: a Jewish man first shared the gospel in Rome; a Roman took it to France; a Frenchman took it to Scandinavia; a Scandinavian to Ireland; an Irishman to Scotland. Every nation where the gospel has been preached had someone travel there from abroad. We serve a God who loves busting borders and knocking down walls. It brings Him great joy when we reach to each other across the distinctions that usually divide us.

Ultimately, whoever you are and wherever you are, it comes down to being honest with yourself. If you are a member of the human race, you must realize you are fallen and can't overcome your sin. Once you realize that, you must be honest enough to acknowledge your need for forgiveness through Christ Jesus. Then, as you begin to follow Him, you will find you must be honest enough to assess your devotion to Him—you'll realize you can never know Him too deeply, never love Him too passionately. And that realization will lead you inevitably to caring about the Great Commission.

When that happens, my friend, the details of your life will fall into place. You'll be amazed how much of God you experience when you give yourself to the things that He cares about. Ask anyone who has ever taken a mission trip; traveling somewhere to serve Him puts your life in a brand-new perspective. Things that seemed so important in your daily life suddenly become insignificant. You're dealing with the destiny of souls now. You're working to enlarge the size of heaven! There is a joy you couldn't have imagined, because you've aligned yourself with the Author of all joy. You will see your family differently. "How can we work together to support the Great Commission?" you'll ask. "Maybe that trip to the beach would be better used on a mission field." You will see your resources differently. *What could I give up*, you will wonder, *so that I could support our friends who are winning people to the Lord?* Never again will you want to simply indulge in your own pleasure— you'll know the joy of returning to God what has always been His. And you will see your church family differently. *We need to send more people on short-term mission projects*, you'll realize. *And we need to help young people realize their calling into career service for God.* You will find yourself stepping forward as a Great Commission encourager, a recruiter and enlister for the army He is raising up. Sooner or later, someone is going to come up to you and say, "You know what? You are *obsessed* with the Great Commission!" And you'll just smile and say, "I know, I know. And I've never been happier. Never been more focused or energetic."

It's time for the days of the Great Omission to end and for us to put aside all the trivia and be about our Father's business. It's simply a matter of self-honesty. It's also a matter of joy, excitement, passion, and adventure.

Do you feel that stirring in your soul? God is moving among

us; I sense it. The needs are so great, and He may be returning soon.

> For the eyes of the LORD range throughout the earth to show Himself strong for those whose hearts are completely His. (2 Chronicles 16:9)

Do you feel His eyes upon you? Do you sense Him sifting your heart to see if it is completely His? Give yourself to Him, this verse tells us, and He will give you His strength. He will show Himself strong in your life, in every way. The adventure will begin.

Then, when this life is over and you cross the border that separates this world from the next, you will be greeted by many, many people. "You don't know me," some stranger will say. "But I heard the gospel because of you, and now I'm here. I've waited here by the gate to thank you." Others will run forward to embrace you, to tell you their stories, and to describe how their eternal destinies were changed forever because of God's power and your obedience. Then one more hand will fall upon your shoulder. You will look at it closely and see the nail marks in it. You will feel the radiance of a smile more powerful than all the suns and stars.

Can you imagine anything more satisfying? Is there any possible reason you wouldn't covet a future like this one? Give up your small ambitions. Be honest with yourself, and choose the future God designed you to live.

The Situation Room

Every pastor has his own pre-worship tradition. A soldier may listen to a special song to help him "get in the zone," or he may strap on his gear in a certain ritualistic way. But the pastor isn't superstitious; he is interested in the zone of special intimacy with God that will help him become the best possible vessel of service to his people that morning. The pastor's study is his "situation room," the place where he seeks his final marching orders before going into spiritual battle. The young pastor may scan his notes, cramming as if it's exam time back in seminary. But as wisdom grows through the years, he finds that prayer is what he really needs. As deeper wisdom comes, he finds ways to enhance that prayer—to be deliberate in the way he comes before the Father, that he may go before the church.

Fifteen years ago, I began to pray through Matthew 28:19–20, asking God to help me preach and lead with the authority mentioned in the Great Commission. I had these verses stenciled on one wall of my office—I had long since memorized them, but I never wanted them to be out of my sight. I would look at those verses on Sunday morning and pray them with all my heart. I didn't want to become inwardly directed, caring only about the members of my own church. On Sunday morning, it's so easy to be consumed by their needs alone. I understood the power of claiming God's promises, so I also took Psalm 2:8 as my own:

Ask of Me,
   and I will make the nations Your inheritance
   and the ends of the earth Your possession.

I asked, "Lord, give me these people. Put the world on my heart. We claim these nations for Jesus Christ!"

I would then turn to praying for my church. Our congregational mission statement, which speaks of reaching Northwest Arkansas and the world, was stenciled on another office wall. I recommitted myself each week to fulfilling that statement in God's power.

On yet another wall, there was a world map. I would then turn to those lands and seas. *There they are,* I thought. *All the lost people who need the gospel shared with them, all the nations where we must go and make disciples.* The map became part of my Sunday morning prayer agenda. It made the Great Commission visual for me.

Pacing the office, praying on my feet, my steps would bring me to a bronze sculpture of Jesus washing the disciples' feet. It spoke to me and found its way into my dialogue with God. "Fill me with humility like this, Lord Jesus. Every knee bows before You, and yet You bow to scrub dirty feet. Every tongue confesses that You are Lord, and yet Your own tongue poured out love and truth for us." Then I would walk over to a picture of my family, the people I love the most deeply in this world. How could I not pray for them—and for all the other families they represented? "Help me to reach families today, dear Lord. Help me connect with them and take them to Jesus." I would come to another little sculpture in my office: a Native American on a horse. I loved the dynamic motion of that hunter, leaning forward with his spear as he galloped, claiming prey to feed his family. He came to represent, for me, the many kinds of faces and world-views out there in the world, the people groups I wouldn't see in our worship center. "God, give me the ability and the opportunity to reach the many beautiful varieties of your children. Red and yellow, black and white, all are precious in Your sight. Help me to reach the ethnic groups of the world."

And then, the globe. It was special to me, too, because it came from Israel. I would return to the Great Commission, where all roads, all avenues of thought and prayer, led for me. I loved the feel of it in my hands as I spun it slowly, letting my fingers glide across Africa and Europe and Asia. I would ask God to show me a nation, show me a continent I might pray for at that moment. As He did, I would place my hand over that portion of the globe and bring it before God. I was struck by the human impossibility of the Great Commission each time I prayed over the globe, but impossible achievements are how God is glorified. "Help me find a way, Lord. Create the medium, the format, that opens that door."

Next, I would focus on the pictures on my wall—photographs of important people for whom I needed to intercede: a picture of George W. Bush was there; after 2008, a souvenir from President Obama's inauguration, given to me by an African-American pastor friend, appeared. It wasn't about whether I bought into their political views, but about the Bible's admonition for me to respect my leaders, submit to them in Christian citizenship, and especially pray for them. I also prayed for such strategic people as James and Shirley Dobson, whose pictures I kept there. "Help me influence and invest in our leaders, O God—political leaders, religious leaders, and international leaders—for the gospel of Jesus Christ."

I would then be ready to walk out the door of my office and join those special men who would pray over me before each service. Those men know how to talk to God, and it was good to bathe in their intercessory prayers for me.

This all became a kind of ritual, but in the best and most powerful sense. It enlarged my vision. While the office décor and the circle of leaders remained, I found that my heart was changing. As I prayed, "Give me the world," I heard and felt a new, recurring whisper:

Ronnie. You can't do it by yourself.

"Well, of course not, Lord, but—"

Ronnie. You can't do it by yourself.

Ten minutes before time for worship, a pastor doesn't want to be wrestling with God. But many times it happens exactly that way—because ten minutes before worship, God tends to have a pastor's undivided attention.

I listened, and during January 2008, my personal mission statement began to change. The new one took me off center stage: "My personal mission is to influence and invest in others to win the world to Christ." In the situation room, the battle was the same one Christians have been fighting for twenty centuries. But this soldier began thinking less in terms of his own movements and more in terms of the army around him.

Once I redirected my prayer on the basis of that change, things began to happen immediately. It's shocking how one puzzle piece can change an entire picture. It's not as if I'd been praying wrongly or without fruit. But if God's Word is the "sword of the Spirit" (Ephesians 6:17),

I had sharpened my weapon. I had gotten closer to the plan He has had all along, and I began to feel Him behind my shoulder, saying, "Now we're getting somewhere, My child!"

In June 2009, I was asked to serve as chairman of the Southern Baptist Convention's Great Commission Resurgence Task Force. One Sunday morning, I was moving through my normal prayer and had come to that *National Geographic* world map. I sensed the Lord speaking to me in my heart, saying, *Ronnie, I am answering your prayer for the nations. What you are doing right now with the Great Commission will affect future generations by placing more missionaries around the world, raising more dollars for the gospel, and equipping more ministers and missionaries than at any time in history.*

Talk about an affirmation! I've already detailed how my world was rocked by what we discovered in that group. What you're holding in your hands, as a matter of fact, is a part of God's answer to my prayer—this book.

And then, something else—something that brought a special smile to my face, one of those fingerprints-of-God moments. I was asked if our church could host a North American Leader's Summit on reaching Native Americans for Christ. I looked at the figure on horseback in my office, and I thanked God for being so good, so faithful—for being always "on the hunt," just like the bronze figure in my office.

I treated myself to a little victory lap around my four walls and all my visual reminders, thanking God all along the way. No, the job was not yet done. The greatest challenges of telling everyone in the world about Jesus and of making disciples of all the nations still lie before us.

But no longer did it seem impossible. God had shown me that the world is really a collection of thousands of people groups—groups such as the one represented by this hunter—and that a vast army of believers is better than one hard-praying soldier. Army by army, and people group by people group, we can win them.

I had asked to be an influencer, an investor in others; and God was giving me all I could handle in answer to that prayer—just as if He'd been waiting for years for me to ask. I was praying more specifically now: to mobilize people, churches, groups, missions, dollars; to reach this people group, that one, groups yet undiscovered.

And the Spirit of God was on the move. Whole new avenues and strategies and formats were opening up every day, across North America and the world.

The situation room was buzzing, and one prayer warrior was finally moving to the front line.

CHAPTER 2

Awaken the Church

One of the first great American authors was Washington Irving, who enjoyed spinning folklore into enduring short stories. "The Legend of Sleepy Hollow," for example, is the quintessential ghost story; "Rip Van Winkle" is a tall tale about a little man who had a big problem with oversleeping.

Rip, we read, is a nice enough man who tends to keep to himself. He's not much interested in village social life. He has attempted to stop the world and get off, mostly by wandering into the Catskill Mountains with his dog, Wolf. There, problems and responsibilities are unlikely to find him. One day Rip wanders a bit too far into the hills, drinks from a stranger's jug, and settles down in the shade of a tree for a nice, long nap. When he awakens, he's a bit surprised by the length of his beard. His dog is gone. And when he walks back into town, the places and the faces are all different. His wife has passed away; his best friends are nowhere to be found. Rip Van Winkle, trying to account for himself to questioning strangers, states that he is a loyal subject of England's King George III, and that doesn't go over the way he expects. The portrait of that George has been replaced in the tavern by a new one—this George bears the last name of Washington. Rip's nap has lasted not twenty minutes, but twenty years. He has gone to sleep in an English colony and awakened in a new nation.[1]

Imagine living during that period, being so geographically close to all the historic events and snoring through them all—the Revolutionary War, the Declaration of Independence, the drafting and ratification of the Constitution, and all the heroics of the Founding Fathers. It's no fun to sleep through all the excitement, is it? But look a little closer at the story. Rip's long nap is really an extension of the values he has carried through life. He has spent a lifetime walking away, not getting involved, avoiding friends and work and even his wife.

I've heard Christian leaders make a troubling comparison between Washington Irving's character and our character as the church of Jesus Christ. They are concerned about our tendency not to engage, to walk away from the real issues of the world. But revolution is occurring all around us even as we yawn away the months and the years. The world has become a global village. Technology has allowed us to communicate in real time with people on the other side of the world. We can turn on our computers and have face time, in real time, with a friend ministering on the streets of Beijing. As I write this, thousands of people in the Middle East are rising up against tyranny for the first time in recorded history in their countries. Revolution is in the air.

Meanwhile, at the local church, we're arguing over new carpet colors for the sanctuary or planning yet another covered-dish dinner. Many of my friends in pastoral ministry are afraid to mention missions in their sermons—they feel the pressure to keep the worship hour peppy, positive, and focused on their members' own interests, not the spiritual needs of those on the other side of the tracks, or the other side of the world. This is an issue we must face: the prevalence of casual Christianity, or as some call it, "easy believism." The church can become just another country club, as we allow people to tell themselves that salvation is a glorified eternal insurance policy that they've purchased. All is forgiven, and the ticket to heaven is punched, so what does it matter how they live right now? If Jesus says, "Take up [your] cross, and follow Me" (Matthew 16:24), can we just write a check and have someone carry it for us?

It's too easy to confuse holiness with a good imitation of it. Yet in Matthew 7:23, Jesus warns us that some people will be shocked at the final judgment when He says to them, "I'm sorry, but I never knew you." These people will be wearing the right Christian T-shirts. They'll have frequented all the trendy Bible study groups, and they are likely to have nothing but contemporary Christian music playing in their earbuds as they wait in line to enter heaven. Imagine one of these fellows getting to the head of the line, smiling confidently, and nodding his head to the beat of his favorite Christian singer. He sees Jesus speaking, so he pulls out his left earbud and says, "Pardon?"

Jesus smiles sadly and repeats, "I'm afraid I don't recognize you."

"But there's got to be some mistake," the fellow says. "I say, 'Lord, Lord!' all the time. Why, I served on committees! I even worked in the nursery once!"

"Can anyone here vouch for you? Show Me some people who are here because you invited them to come."

The fellow turns a little pale because he can't think of a single person.

Jesus said we would be known by our fruits: "Every branch in Me that does not produce fruit He removes" (John 15:2).

Are we telling people this in our sermons? Do we need to listen more carefully to all Jesus said, and not just the comfortable parts? If so, we're going to conclude that He takes fruit bearing very, very seriously.

A Church Grown Flabby

George Barna heads a polling and research group that specializes in findings about spirituality and people's views of the church. Recently Barna's organization completed five thousand interviews from which they isolated six great themes:

1. Theological literacy is plummeting in the church.
2. Churches are becoming more ingrown and less interested in reaching out to others.
3. Members want "practical" formulas rather than profound spiritual truth.
4. Christians are showing more interest in community action.
5. The postmodern insistence on tolerance is gaining ground quickly among Christians.
6. Christianity is having near-zero impact on the surrounding culture.[2]

I can't say I'm surprised by any of these conclusions. It's not that I'm cynical or a know-it-all; it's just that after thirty-four years in church ministry, my eyes are open. I see these things coming to pass. I've served at my current church for more than two decades, and I know our congregation is no more immune than any other. We're feeling the steady undertow of a worldly, post-Christian culture—and that breaks my heart. In short, as George Barna's reams of data are telling us—and our observations are affirming—we are a church in crisis.

If today's evangelical church were personified as an ordinary man, we would find him flabby and out of shape. He would once have had a good and fulfilling daily job. His work made the world a better place, which made him glow with satisfaction as he came home each evening to rest before another wonderful day of work. He felt the impact he was making. But somewhere along the way, he became more interested in relaxing. He built a nice home-theater system, and he began watching so much television that he increasingly forgot the great work at the center of his life. Much of the time he no longer even reported in at the office, and the world began to resent him a little bit. The world looked at him and said, "You don't care very much about us, do you? It's all about you." He hears that, he feels that, and he is sad about it. He is a good man, but one who simply lost his way. He's not sure how to turn things back around again.

But there is a way to do it. We could reverse the slippage. Throughout church history, there have been times when the people of God were caught up in the work of the Holy Spirit. Revivals would spring up, one place after another. Things would begin to happen in surrounding communities—good things. Child labor would be banned; slavery would be eliminated. Schools would be started, poor people would find jobs, hungry people would be fed, and the bottom would fall out of crime rates. Christianity has changed the world more than once—it has done it over and over.

But the darkness is stubborn, and it always creeps back in as the candle begins to flicker. We have one last great hope, and if we are going to fulfill it, we need to take a stone-cold-sober look at what Barna is telling us:

- We *must* be literate in the things of God.
- We *must* rediscover our passion for those outside the church walls.

- We *must* walk away from fluffy self-help and resume preaching the true gospel.
- We *must* counter the comfortable illusions of tolerance with the plain facts of eternal life and judgment.
- We *must* expand our reach from community action to worldwide discipleship.
- We *must* once again discover what Jesus means when He commands us to be salt and light in the world; a city situated on a hill (Matthew 5:13–14); a guiding influence upon human culture rather than one more entrée in the smorgasbord of opinions.

There was a prophet named Joel who lived twenty-five hundred years ago but who spoke to our time even as he addressed his own. Joel's message was that casual godliness is a contradiction in terms, a sign that something is deeply wrong. It is the precursor to judgment—as Joel called it, the day of the Lord. Joel spoke of impending danger but also beckoning hope. We are always a prayer away, a repentant heart away from finding our way home again.

Plagues came in Joel's time—swarms of locusts and invading soldiers. It's a pattern that reaches back to the book of Judges and forward throughout history: when we fall into spiritual slumber and surrender to worldliness, we weaken ourselves until we are easy prey. Devastation always arrives. Joel isolates the precious attainments that are lost through our spiritual complacency, then and now.

Every follower of Jesus Christ needs to read the three short chapters of the book of Joel and apply its message to his or her life. We need to reflect upon what Joel is saying to our churches and to our nation. The frightening truth is that God doesn't change. The Bible is a book of history for the very reason that it is also a book of prophecy. What God has done, He always will do.

What We Lose

Spiritual complacency brings devastation we never see coming. It could be compared to allowing termites to eat at the foundation of a house. For a time, things seem secure. The damage will be found much too late.

The Loss of Protection

Joel's generation compromised their worship of God by revering competing nations, ideologies, and idols. Compromise always leads to weakness, because we lose the strength that comes through the purity of commitment. God told the people they should be grieving over their plight, as a young virgin would grieve at the news that her fiancé has died. The church, of course, is the bride of Christ. While He will never die, we allow our relationship with Him to succumb to slow death. And when that happens, indeed we should be grieving for what we have lost.

In our day, too, competing ideologies have set up shop in the very shadows of our steeples. We view Christ not as the way, the truth, and the life, but as one option among any number of equal ones. And even among those who choose Jesus, there is a tendency to bend and shape Him to personal preferences, rather than bend behavior to His will. Given that viewpoint, is it any wonder that people grow casual in their commitment? If Jesus is just a matter of personal taste, why should we devote ourselves completely to Him?

Joel suggests to us that the loss of passion for God means the forfeiture of protection from God. America is in free fall, just as Judah was in Joel's day.

The Loss of Provision

The locusts came, and the locusts consumed. There was no harvest in Israel. It's hard for us to imagine the panic and despair that sets into an agrarian world when the agriculture falls into shambles. No wonder Joel said that the land itself grieved over its sickness and that the people should join in mourning. Starvation is a horrible future to embrace.

People everywhere have always looked to heaven and prayed for the Lord's provision. Our Thanksgiving holiday enshrines the concept of giving thanks for the food God provides. We think of the early American settlers facing a bitter winter in a strange land with little but their faith in the God who led them across the ocean.

Modern American culture is smug about its provision. God is no longer seen as necessary, because technology giveth and technology taketh away. Everything results from just the random interactions of so many chemicals. The only problem is that when the cupboards are bare, you can't pray to technology. Our last great hope is realizing that God reigns, that all good gifts come from Him and can be removed as a measure of loving discipline, just as a parent may send a child to bed without dinner.

What's the truth about the economic collapse of the last few years? Is it explainable strictly by market forces? (Note that we often attribute personal characteristics to the economy, as if it were a living god: the market "responds"; it "makes corrections"; it "loves" this and is "fickle" because of that.) Or could God have His hands on the financial reins? Perhaps these times represent a call to His people to heed the warning of Jesus: "Don't collect for yourselves treasures on earth, where moth and rust destroy and where thieves break in and steal. But collect for yourselves treasures in heaven" (Matthew 6:19–20).

The Loss of Joy

The last phrase in Joel 1:12 is immeasurably sad: "Indeed, human joy has dried up."

36

These are the words of a world in which all was lost. There was no food, no security, no spiritual consolation, no hope. By losing God, they lost all. All the nation had left was the richness of its collective memory, its history. Nobody could take that away. But to live with nothing but memory is to live in despair, which is the opposite of joy. Life becomes a funeral without end, which is the way Joel describes things as he calls on the nation to dress in sackcloth and mourn (1:8).

Joy flows like a fountain for those who drink deeply from the living water that is life with Christ. This joy can't be dimmed by circumstances. We may not be happy, but we have joy deep within us. It doesn't ultimately matter how dark the darkness is because light will always overcome it. But in our churches are faces filled with gloom. Somehow God's people have forgotten the way to that fountain. They are parched, even as hope is so very near. The church is in crisis, as Joel's land of Judah was in crisis. It's a frightening time, but is there hope?

Yes!

You Snooze, You Lose

The remedy for falling asleep on the job is simple: *wake up!*

I tend to rise early in the morning, but I live in fear of oversleeping, just like everyone else. One alarm clock simply isn't enough for me to have confidence. What happens if I hit the p.m. button instead of the a.m.? What happens if the clock fails to do its duty? I need another clock to get the first clock's back! I sleep a little better knowing the two of them are both on the job.

Alarm Number One sounds at 3:00 a.m. And yes, there is a snooze button, and I'm very aware of its powers as I reach for that clock at that hour. I know better—but I'm tempted. Since I've built my schedule around having those early hours, I'm going to be frustrated later on if I lose out on them. So I'm going to grit my teeth and bypass that snooze button. I may not be happy for the next two or three minutes, but I'm going to tough it out and pry my eyelids open. It's not my favorite moment of the day, but it's the first battle, and I'm determined to win it. So often, as goes the first battle, so goes the war.

Joel calls upon his nation of Judah to awaken. The people have fallen into spiritual slumber, and they need to open their eyes—*now*. To say, "We'll clean up our act next year," would be to hit the snooze button, roll over, and inch closer to catastrophe. Have you noticed? The day doesn't postpone itself until we get up; it goes right on, and the time we snooze is the time we lose. What Judah stood to lose were serious things. They lost their protection, their provision, and their joy. So it's time to awaken from the nightmare.

I wonder how many of us need the spiritual wake-up call. How many of us believe God's blessings are an entitlement because we were raised as Christians, because we live in a supposedly Christian nation, or because of some other reason? We can't get around the fact that God has numbered our days, time is currency, and He holds us accountable for how we spend it. Rip Van Winkle's story is a fantasy, but I've known too many people who have said, "I'll make things right with God later," and the next thing they know, twenty years have gone by. Soon they've lost their friends, and they can no longer communicate with their spouses. Then they find that the picture of the King, which once hung in their hearts, has been replaced by something else.

You snooze, you lose. And what you lose might forever slip from your grasp.

Get Up and Go

Getting out of bed is the start of the battle, but after that, it's important to get going. Action drives away the final hold that sleep has on us. Joel wanted his people to awaken and hit the ground running, and he didn't mince words. Some preachers today are prone to sugarcoating the message, but the prophets of old were anything but diplomatic. When the house is burning down, you don't seek out a book of etiquette so you can phrase every word correctly as you inform others of the flames. You shout instructions—and that's what Joel did. He called on the priests to spend the night in sackcloth, howling in sorrow for the altar that was without a sacrifice. Nothing was happening in the temple, which meant God and His children were out of touch. Joel also commanded the priests to call a sacred (or solemn) assembly and begin a time of fasting, prayer, and crying out to God (1:13–15).

Do you know the best remedy for spiritual dryness? Action. People too often lead with their emotions. They think, *I'll pray when I feel closer to God. I'll get back to church when I feel the need*. But emotions beget themselves. The temporary stagnation becomes a permanent condition when we let it be. It's far more powerful and effective to act your way into feeling, rather than to feel your way into acting. We kneel when we pray because we lead with action, and the spirit follows the body. We fast because the emptiness makes us feel the need for fullness in God. The priests donned sackcloth and spread ashes on their faces because it helped them to feel what they needed to feel as they cried out to God. They gathered the people because this wasn't simply a priest problem; it was a people problem. It was a time for the community to come together, realize the depth of the crisis, and turn to the only hope of salvation. Churches today still hold sacred or solemn assemblies. It's a time to call people to repentance and renewal. To repent is to turn fully away from sin, call it what it is, renounce it, and walk in the other direction.

There has never been a country that glorifies individuality as the United States does. We speak of faith as a personal matter, and we uphold personal freedoms as sacred—and rightly so. But faith is also a community matter. As John Donne wrote, no man is an island—but each of us is part of the social whole.[3] There are times when we need to come together in a spirit of prayer and repentance. God looks upon us not only as individuals, but also as churches, nations, and groupings of all kinds. Our last great hope involves pulling our spiritual communities together for the sacred business of coming clean before God, recognizing sin where we find it, confessing, and feeling the joy of His forgiveness. We need to wake up individually and collectively. We need to throw off the sin that has entangled us and run toward God's throne to rededicate ourselves.

As I've reflected on the urgency of these things, I've returned to a book of mine called *The Power of Prayer and Fasting: God's Gateway to Spiritual Breakthroughs*, revised and expanded it.[4] Fasting is certainly a subject unto itself, and I recommend you get from that book the details on how you and your church can approach fasting and repentance.

Has your church held a solemn assembly lately? Many, I'm afraid, wouldn't be familiar with the terminology. The assembly can be life changing not only for individuals, but for whole churches. I'm glad that so many churches do a good job of celebration in typical worship services, but balance is an important consideration. There should be moments of deep conviction, of humility in the presence of God. We can miss those, if we're not careful, amid the loud sound and guitar solos. There is "a time to weep and a time to laugh; a time to mourn and a time to dance" (Ecclesiastes 3:4). In the solemn assembly, there is Scripture reading, there is prayer, and there is silence. We come before our Lord and pray for spiritual awakening. We beseech God as our first and last great hope. It is a time of brokenness and a time of mending; a time that quiets the soul, sets things in their proper perspective, and seeks the outset of revival.

The beauty of holding a solemn assembly in your church is that for once, you don't need that powerful mixing board and sound system. The band can sit in the congregation with everyone else, in prayer and reflection. You don't need to prepare a sermon—just prepare your heart. The young and the old can stand up to read a verse, to lead a prayer, to take part in what the Holy Spirit is doing.

Let's think of the heart of God when we come together, solemn and quiet, for such a time. How would you respond if you were a parent and your children came to you solemnly, dedicating themselves to putting away their disobedience and devoting themselves to being your children? God softens His heart to us when we focus on repentance. His Spirit flows among us in an incredibly powerful way, and we come away with a renewed sense of devotion.

If you're heartbroken over the state of your church, don't give up hope. God can do more in a moment than we could do in a lifetime. He doesn't want to see your church die of spiritual thirst. He is longing for His children to come running into His arms. Maybe He's moving at this very moment in the depth of your soul, nudging you to step forward and request a solemn assembly for your congregation.

Seize the Day

Think about the feeling you have when you win the wake-up battle early in the morning. You rise, you shower and dress, and you step out onto the patio, a mug of hot coffee in your hand. There's something special, something holy about the freshness of a new morning, isn't there? You are ready and rested, at your best, and the sun is beginning to shine. You're aware of the incredible opportunities that beckon with the new day.

This is the feeling when a church awakens from its slumber. It rubs its eyes; it feels strong when it has only felt weary; it looks out upon the world with a surge of adrenaline. So much to do! So much power in the Holy Spirit! You feel pulled forward, as a hunter feels when the dogs strain at the leash, eager to run across the meadow.

This is the time of opportunity, the time for action. Paul the apostle described a great awakening in Romans 13:11: "Besides this, knowing the time, it is already the hour for you to wake up from sleep, for now our salvation is nearer than when we first believed."

For you or for me, "knowing the time" is a matter of glancing at a watch. But in the vocabulary of Scripture, the meaning is very different. Paul chooses a Greek word that refers to a special moment in history in the fullness of time—a defining moment. This kind of time is a point of convergence when history, circumstances, individuals, and God's ongoing plan all come together by destiny. I believe Paul would apply that word to these times. This is a defining moment when the Spirit of God is acting within us to take the gospel to all nations and make disciples everywhere. All paths have led to this crossroads, and we must choose our steps wisely. Sin is rampant, but so is wonderful opportunity. The devil is on the prowl, but the Spirit is on the move. *Carpe diem*—"seize the day."

Thus the once and future message of Joel is to wake up, get moving, and take hold of the opportunities before us. The greater the spiritual crisis, the greater the glory for God's name when He wins the victory.

Sound the Alarm

Alarms go off at the strangest times. We've had the fire alarm sound at home—a false alarm, but it didn't stop the fire trucks from piling into our neighborhood. We've had alarms set off at church too. One time it happened right before a wedding. We had a short delay, calmed everyone down, and picked up where we left off. It's a nerve-jangling moment. Nobody likes alarms, because they're not designed to function as beautiful music; they're designed to grab your urgent attention. They're loud, shrill, and when they finally stop, we sigh in relief. But as unwelcome as that sound might be, it might just save your life.

Joel opens the second chapter of his book with these words:

> Blow the horn in Zion;
>> sound the alarm on My holy mountain! (2:1)

From that height, I suppose an alarm could carry a long way—something like an air-raid signal. Joel and the other prophets are God's emergency warning systems. Like alarms, the words of the prophets are loud, abrasive, and often disturbing. Like our stubborn smoke detectors that we tend to pound, the prophets even take beatings in their audiences' attempts to silence them and preserve the status quo. Are we sure we need to shut off the alarm? It depends upon how much credence we give to the warning. Some of Joel's generation listened, took heed, and cleaned up their acts. Others cursed and went back to sleep. Here is God's alarming message, then and now.

Judgment Is Coming

Judgment in the Bible is always a now-and-later thing. Through our sin we begin, in the here and now, to reap what we have sown. This is the judgment we bring upon ourselves because of the way God has designed the universe. He has created moral order, just as He has established physical order, so that when we violate His principles, we bring misery upon ourselves. The prophet can always say, "Look around you! Aren't you already seeing the implications of your life decisions?" But nothing blinds people as easily as their own sin does. The truth is so disturbing that they seek to explain it away and go back to sleep. As I write these words, one more Hollywood star is all over the media, attempting to justify his self-destructive lifestyle. "The heart is more deceitful than anything else and desperately sick—who can understand it?" (Jeremiah 17:9). Sin has this policy: "Pay me now *and* pay me later."

We break the laws of God at the early juncture, but God Himself will have His say, on a day sinners would rather miss. Joel has a name for this occasion: the day of the Lord. All of us have reserved seats for this main event. The loose ends of history will all be tied up, all accounts will be balanced, and history will reach its final moment. Only one question will be considered on that day: how do we stand with the Son of God?

Doesn't the realization that there is such a day, and that it could come at any time, make you feel that the alarm should be sounded from the highest mountain of every nation? Shouldn't it be shouted in every city street and down every road where even a solitary individual lives? It's an alarm of dire warning, but also of joyful, wonderful news. There is judgment, but there is also Jesus. The offer of salvation is for everyone with ears to hear and an eternity to consider. It is the offer of heaven itself.

The alarm, heard rightly, becomes the sound of Easter bells tolling the news that someone has already paid a terrible price for every sin we ever committed; He suffered a humiliating death then rose again in victory, so that we need never live in fear of what lies beyond this life. As a matter of fact, He invites us into His kingdom as full heirs, to live forever in the fulfillment of absolute joy, with all tears and sadness wiped away. Bells can toll for a funeral or a new birth. We decide which outcome they foretell.

An Outpouring of the Spirit

Joel speaks, amazingly enough, of events that will come to pass long after his time on earth. He tells of the coming of the Holy Spirit. God says, "I will pour out My Spirit on all humanity" (2:28). He describes it as a time of wonder, when even slaves would feel the Spirit of God within them, when sons and daughters would prophesy, and when old men would dream dreams. All the lost things—the provision and protection, the joy of salvation—would be restored due to hearts returning to their Creator. The Spirit of the Lord would wash over humanity in a great outpouring, and then the day of the Lord would dawn.

The next phase of Joel's timetable, of course, was to be seen in the events described in Acts 2—the day of Pentecost, when the Spirit of God descended and the people began moving among the nations to share the good news of Jesus Christ. We await the culmination of this prophecy as the gospel is preached to all the world and the power and presence of God is poured out upon people of every nation. Paul describes what happens when people hear and accept the gospel: "In Him you also, when you heard the word of truth, the gospel of your salvation—in Him when you believed—were sealed with the promised Holy Spirit" (Ephesians 1:13).

The Spirit seals us, marking us as God's forgiven children forever, and the day of the Lord is no longer an event to fear, but a time of personal rejoicing. It will be a day when the gospel will spread like wildfire.

The New Testament uses two images to describe the movement of the Holy Spirit: wind and fire. When those two things come together, you have a massive conflagration. The wonderful wildfire of godly passion will be a global event, one that will be a wonder to observe.

Harvesttime

Finally, the alarm resounds to tell us that it is harvesttime. Joel's contemporaries knew what it meant to bring in a harvest, but this will be a harvest of human souls, finally complete as history reaches its climax. We've seen the Great Awakening, the Second Great Awakening, and many great revivals throughout the annals of Western civilization. They have changed the world, but all of them must pale in comparison to the final events of our mission to take the gospel to the world and make disciples. The world, from its billions of people, will yield its final crop of souls; "then everyone who calls on the name of Yahweh will be saved" (Joel 2:32).

What will that be like? It will be global revival on the scale of a megamovement. People in every nation, and of every station, will see the goodness of God and the wickedness of their ways in bright contrast. Among these people, there will be sorrowful weeping as people realize and repent of their sin. And among them, every knee will bow and every tongue will confess that Jesus is Lord. The churches, of course, will be too small to take in the surging crowds—it would be like teacups trying to contain the ocean. We have to think that schools, halls, stadiums, and assembly facilities of every kind will be packed to capacity with people who have come to pray and beseech God. The streets will be teeming with new believers in search of guidance. These people will call upon His name, and He will answer their call as He always has—embracing them in His great arms, drying their tears, restoring their joy. Even as this incredible event comes to pass, the sun will be setting on earth's final day. Heaven will be near, and judgment will come. Such will be the great harvest.

We would all love to be able to put the event on our calendars, but Jesus warns about seeking to know the times or seasons. James points out that we don't know what tomorrow may bring and that every moment of life is given by the grace of God (4:14). We can only live in humility and obedience. God will do what He will do, regardless of whether you or I get involved. But who wouldn't want to be a part of His great work? We need to wake up the church. We've slept too long, and we've attended to too much trivia. It's time for us to get up, move into action, and seize the day. The fields, Jesus says, are white unto harvest, and they need workers (John 4:35).

Are you ready to begin?

Lessons from Kudzu

Kudzu—it's a Southern thing.

Back in 1883, a strange Chinese vine was introduced at the New Orleans Exposition. It was said to prevent soil erosion and do all kinds of other wonderful things.

But mostly what it did was multiply itself. In a little over a century, it has taken over yards, forests, and roadsides all over the Southeast, and it can't be stopped. They say that the first year it sleeps; the second it creeps; the third it leaps!

Kudzu isn't attractive or popular, but it has lessons to teach us. In the beginning, the church grew in a similar way. Jesus had said, "I am the vine; you are the branches. The one who remains in Me and I in him produces *much fruit*" (John 15:5, emphasis added). The growth was dramatic, exponential.

But along the way, our imagery changed—from vine to vain. People began building church *buildings*. Beautiful cathedrals, which soared into the sky, were built to last a thousand years, and they were assembled, brick by brick, by generations of families.

Europe is filled with empty towers, lovely as they are, intended for the glory of God. And to this day, if you ask a lot of people to define *church*, they will tell you it is a building. Something made of cold bricks and pretty glass.

Buildings are good. They happen to be necessary

most of the time, and they even have the ability to inspire us to excellence in worshipping and serving God. In Northwest Arkansas, we have built beautiful church campuses, and we're grateful for them.

But we understood all along that architecture was not our destiny. We didn't want to build a monument for tourists to come and visit someday. Bricks, glass—these things will perish, but people are forever. They are headed for one of two destinations, and we wanted to mobilize to take as many as possible to the best one.

From 1993 to 2000, Cross Church, where I am pastor, invested in and planted eleven churches regionally, nationally, and internationally. That was a start, but it was never intended to represent the finish line.

In 2001, our own growth as a church necessitated our becoming a multisite church. By the wisdom of some, that would have been a great time to pull in our focus and emphasize the home front and the challenge of multiple campuses. Few would have criticized that approach.

Instead, we went the other way. We invested in and planted forty-four churches regionally, nationally, and internationally between 2001 and 2010, adding up to a total of fifty-five churches in seventeen years, from nearby to across the globe—at least one on every inhabited continent.

We presented, discussed, and committed to a three-year vision called "Greater Things." Every member of our church knows that this is what we're about: fifty more churches regionally, nationally, and internationally over the next three years.

This is to happen at the same time when we're mobilizing at least one thousand church members to experience a cross-cultural missions experience outside Northwest Arkansas. Consider, also, that during the worst economic slump in living memory, our people have committed multiple millions of dollars—over and above the normal church budget—toward these goals.

Things are shaking at Cross Church! It's also true that God has a way of showing up and doing amazing things we never expected, simply because we're attempting to be obedient. We've received gifts, opportunities, and blessings as never before. God is good.

But what about the people? Do they go for an aggressive Great Commission focus as opposed to church ministry that focused more on their felt needs? Donnie Smith, CEO and president of Tyson Foods, told one reporter, "I've been a member of Cross Church for twenty-three years, and I can tell you I've never felt more closely aligned to our church's strategic direction."[5] He plans on taking his family on a mission trip to Malawi, part of our Greater Things initiative, and I can tell you that he has a Great Commission heart pumping inside him.

There are a lot of people like Donnie Smith where I live. It's not something in the Arkansas water; it's something in the gospel, something that happens inside us when suddenly our priorities fall into line with those of our Lord. If you would like to see powerful change in the people in your church, it's just a matter of getting them to want the things God wants.

Back to our church-planting schedule. I hope you can see that Cross Church's pattern has been one of acceleration—a pattern of urgency—and also of taking on greater goals as we develop greater competency:

11 churches in 7 years
44 churches in 10 years
50 churches in 3 years

The aggressive "fifty" number coincides with starting a new campus. For us, it's both/and, not either/or. It's not here *or* there, it's everywhere!

This is a scriptural principle: God giving us charge of greater things as we show our faithfulness in smaller ones. I want the time to come when we consider planting fifty churches in the "smaller things" category compared to what we later accomplished!

I describe in chapter 8 how I developed a burden to bypass cherished ministries—a national television broadcast, for example—because we felt that, at that time, there were simply better, wiser ways to be faithful with our resources of time and money and people. There are many ways to spend money and spin wheels. We could put tremendous effort into some kind of special event, invite people from all over the world to come to Arkansas for it, and I know God would bless that. But I also suspect it would be big news today, old news tomorrow. Someone else would soon be throwing another big shindig in yet another place.

But plant one healthy gospel church? Plant ten? Plant a hundred? I know we can change eternal destinations that way. I know that people yet unborn, not to mention reborn, could come to know Christ someday in the future through the churches we plant today.

Maybe we would discover that we could only plant one thousand churches over a certain period, when we wanted five times that many. God has His own goals;

it could be that one of those plants would become the most wildly fruitful branch in Christian history. We just can't anticipate the good things God will do; all we can do is be obedient in the here and now. And that's what I'm pleading with church leaders to do.

In my denomination, we have more than 45,700 churches. In 2010, all those churches together planted 1,271 new congregations.[6] Sadly, the number of churches we will see *die* during the year is a similar total—so our net gain will be small. This is why, in our Great Commission Resurgence effort, we reset the priority of the North American Mission Board, focusing at least 50 percent of its efforts, finances, and missionaries toward planting healthy, multiplying gospel churches in America.

It's an uncomfortable truth, but God will hold us accountable. To whom so much has been given, much is now required. We need to be starting hundreds of thousands of new, evangelical, gospel-driven churches— many more than the total number now existing. It sounds fantastic, but in truth it's our last great hope. We must burst into full bloom, or we will wilt into yesterday's dust.

It's time, then, to stop focusing on building cathedrals and start focusing on planting. The gospel will take root in every culture, it will spread powerfully, and we will see the Great Commission fulfilled.

But it won't happen until we stop talking and start planting. And we must all do it together. Cross Church needs to join hands with your church, and with churches all across the world. Simply read the New Testament to see the pattern. This was what Paul and all his associates did; it was in the DNA of the New Testament church.

What goals will your church set? How many churches

will your congregation plant locally, nationally, and internationally over the next few years? The next decade? Will you set humble, "realistic" goals that everyone agrees are doable? (It's okay to start with just one and then branch out from there—as long as you just do it!) Or will you set prayerfully aggressive, humanly impossible goals that excite and energize people for the very reason that they are visionary?

It's time for us to put away our little ideas, stop dreaming of little futures, and stop playing little church. God is on the move. Great things are coming. People are awakening to the mission He has had for us all along.

Perhaps God is calling you right now, even as you read these words, to begin the dialogue that will transform your church into a Great Commission–planting fellowship.

CHAPTER 3

Accept the Urgency

urgent: *requiring or compelling speedy action or attention*

Christmas. New York City. I'd always dreamed of having both at the same time. In 2010, Jeana and I finally looked at each other and said, "Let's make it happen." So, after the morning service on the Sunday following Thanksgiving, we packed our bags and climbed onto a plane. We had three days to take in a Big Apple Christmas season.

What is it with me and big cities? I love them, and I always have. Don't get me wrong: Springdale, Arkansas, is right where God wants me, and I feel privileged to call it home. But I often wonder why God never dropped me into a true urban setting; I certainly have a passion for the cities. The swarms of humanity, the tall skyscrapers, and the raw energy seem to throw my spirit into overdrive.

So I was thrilled to be in the quintessential Big City in late

November 2010. We shopped in the well-known stores, enjoyed some fine dining, and did some serious people watching—the crowds coming and going, men and women and children taking for granted their roles in the NYC experience.

We arrived early for the lighting of the massive Christmas tree at Rockefeller Plaza and watched as several streets were closed off to accommodate the crowds.

"There they are," said Jeana. "The NYPD." A number of city police were on hand, making sure things went smoothly.

"I was watching them too," I replied. "Notice how young they are?" It was true. There weren't many crusty old cops here, but mostly young men and women.

I thought one more time about the event that still hung in the New York air, and probably always will—the terrorist attacks of September 11, 2001. How many of these fresh, young faces were there on that morning? How many of them were among the heroes who rushed into the doomed towers on their terrifying rescue missions? Members of the police force, fire department, and other emergency units paid the ultimate price on that awful day. Just under 3,000 people died, 411 of whom were rescue workers. And few of them were taken by surprise. They knew that by running in, they might not live to run out. They had been trained for just such a time, of course, but the moment of need is always the proving ground for bravery. In the NYC rescue workers, raw courage and dedication were revealed. As with most Americans, I have reserved a small piece of my heart for them for as long as I live.

Jeana and I stood quietly in tribute, watching the police and reflecting on these things. Tonight's occasion was a calm one: a tree-lighting ceremony, family time. There was no particular sense of urgency in these preparations. How different from that Tuesday morning nine years earlier. The emergency of 9/11 materialized quickly, incredibly, and there was no time to think or plan or debate—just to rescue lives, as many and as quickly as possible.

Urgency. That's the word for a moment of supreme clarity, of surging adrenaline. Any other time, we have any number of subjects revolving through our minds. Then, in the moment of decision, there is only one thing that matters, one thing to confront. And the stakes tend to be very high.

Most of us know the death count from 9/11, but we'll never know the life count. How many were saved by the sense of urgency manifest in the NYC rescue workers? What might the death toll have been if the rescuers hadn't been prepared or hadn't taken the threat seriously?

If you have picked up on a sense of urgency in my writing, then you've been paying attention. I believe the message of the Bible that tells us there is a heaven and a hell. I believe that the sacrificial life, death, and resurrection of Jesus Christ have made it possible for as many people to be rescued as we are willing to attempt. I believe there are limitations of time and opportunity, and that the vital signs of the world and the church indicate that we have one last great hope—to awaken the Great Commission in all His disciples. Therefore I have a sense of urgency, and I want to recruit other rescue workers who share it. The task is staggering: to present the gospel to every corner of this planet and to make disciples of the nations. With such a colossal goal and so little time, we need millions of committed, Spirit-filled Christians working together with a passion for evangelism and a dedication never to stop until we have finally obeyed the command of Jesus.

The comparison to the rescues of September 11, 2001, is an apt one, but the rescues of the Great Commission are more critical—souls in the billions instead of thousands. The problem is that CNN isn't covering this rescue situation. Most of the world has no idea that lives—eternal lives—are in the balance. Even for the church, it's business as usual rather than an earnest, courageous rush to do the work of God while there is still time.

As Jeana and I watched the police, I also wondered, *How many of them need rescuing?* Did I feel a sense of urgency for someone to share the gospel with them? With the people around us in the crowd? With the food servers and shop cashiers and flight attendants we'd seen in the last day or so? I stood with my hands in my pockets and tried to imagine these police, with their own hands in their own pockets, on 9/11. What if the news cameras had shown them rubbernecking as the buildings burned, as people leaped from ninety floors above? What if the rescue workers had been casual spectators rather than courageous heroes? And I thought, *What does God see when He looks at me? at my church? at the Christians of this world?* We're just a vast number of Planet Earth rescue workers with our hands in our pockets, gawking as the earth goes up in flames.

Of course, the rescue crew was very successful on September 11. Thanks be to God that they were. Now I want to be successful too. I want all of us to feel a sense of urgency, to rush into the fire to rescue souls, as many and as quickly as possible.

What's the greatest difference between the churches of the first century and those of the twenty-first century? Is it technology? Big buildings? No, the most critical difference is the sense of urgency. Read the book of Acts, and you come to the conclusion that Paul and his partners did missions as if their hair were on fire. But today we might spend several years planting one new church and feel good about our efforts. In spite of language barriers, no curricula, no seminars, and no handbooks, the first-generation Christians planted churches in the soil constantly; and they counted on the Holy Spirit to do the watering.

All it took was the Spirit of God, their own spiritual gifts, and the sense of urgency. In their correspondences, preserved for us in the New Testament, they referred frequently to the return of Jesus and the coming judgment. To them, since Jesus could come back anytime, it followed that they should try to save Jews and non-Jews, as many and as quickly as possible.

Our urgency has six dimensions: theological, spiritual, physical, statistical, strategic, and personal. As we examine each one, we'll begin to gain a better grasp of how deep a problem we face.

Theologically Urgent

As Christians, we draw our theology from the Scriptures, the authority in all theological matters. I evaluate any issue by first asking, "What does the Bible say?" I cannot escape from its truth, particularly on creation, salvation, and eternity. I will make the following three items brief and simple, although each could be a one-thousand-page theological treatise.

Special Creation

The Bible tells us in Genesis 1–3 that we are God's special and distinct creation. He made us in His image as male and female, and He gave us dominion over the earth. He also implanted within us the freedom to choose. We were a perfect creation, but we forfeited that creation by using our freedom to choose disobedience. On that day, we became slaves to sin rather than children of God.

Salvation

God provided for our salvation through His Son, who gave His life to take the punishment we earned on the day we freely chose disobedience. By acknowledging and accepting the free gift of salvation through Jesus and His work on the cross, we can be saved despite our sinful rebellion. We also know that Jesus is the one and only provision—that apart from Him, we face an eternity of punishment for those same sins.

Eternity

The Bible affirms the existence of both heaven and hell. Those at peace with God spend a perfect eternity in His presence, but those who have not accepted Jesus' free gift of salvation must face an eternity of punishment. Each of us must personally make the decision about his or her eternal status.

Those are the bare bones of Christianity, and they tell us how imperative it is to present the gospel to every person in the world and make disciples of all nations. If we don't agree, then we simply haven't been listening. Or perhaps there is a hole in our gospel somewhere: we've missed that Jesus is the only way; we've missed that there is eternal accountability; we've missed that the Bible means what it says and these essentials are not open for interpretation. True and complete theology instills a sense of urgency.

Spiritually Urgent

As a young boy, I once traveled with my family to Houston, Texas. We wanted to visit a nice shopping mall there. After the two-hour trip, we walked into the mall and I promptly became lost. At my age, I'd never been in such a place, never known the perils of getting lost in such a commercial hub. Once the reality of my lostness sank in, I began to cry uncontrollably. It's frightening to know you're lost. What if some stranger took me away? What if I never saw my family again?

Do we understand that those without Christ are lost in a much more frightening sense? They aren't embracing alternative philosophies—they're lost. Their eternal fates hang in the balance.

Have you forgotten what it means to be without Christ, without bearings? First, it means spiritual death. Ephesians 2:1 describes your past as "dead in your trespasses and sins." Did you realize your soul was lifeless, a dead thing? Did you feel the utter emptiness? Second, it means spiritual lostness. Do you know what it means to be in the middle of the sea without a compass or a rudder while the stars are hidden? You are aimless, with no destination, no sense of spiritual location. If you are honest, you must admit that life ultimately lacks meaning. It has no point; you have no point.

Those who are lost won't remain so. They have a concrete destination. We know it as hell. As Christians who trust the Bible, we affirm this and scorn the universalists who believe there is no hell and no judgment. But the sad truth is that we live just like them. If we truly believed that our friends, our family members, and the people all around us stood on the precipice of eternal suffering, we would be moved to speak up about it. That is, we would feel a sense of urgency.

Again we remember the images of people throwing themselves from the upper floors of the World Trade Center. Those pictures are terrifying, tragic. But how much worse is the idea of millions upon millions of people plummeting toward an eternity of punishment? Only in Christ do they have hope for rescue. Only through us will they hear about it.

Physically Urgent

I've seen a great deal of change in my corner of Arkansas. There were fewer people living here when I first arrived. The daily newspaper reflected peaceful communities where deaths were mainly limited to illness and old age. I rarely saw much evidence of crime. But with the growth of the population has come a rise in tragic and untimely death—from crime or other reasons. Young couples are victims. Children die. What I'm seeing is what the Bible affirms:

> You don't even know what tomorrow will bring—what your life will be! For you are a bit of smoke that appears for a little while, then vanishes. (James 4:14)

If tomorrow is so uncertain, what does that say about today? This is the time—the only sure time—for us to rescue the perishing. Hebrews 9:27 tells us,

> It is appointed for people to die once—and after this, judgment.

The 1960s' Schlitz Beer commercial actually had it right: we only come around once in life. But instead of grabbing "for all the gusto [we] can get," we should be less selfish about it. We don't want to sit around drinking beer; we want to grab for all of God's children we can reach and ensure a joyous eternity for them.

There is a physical urgency because death is the end of the opportunity to use our free wills. In this life, all our decisions will be final. I've been around the world and seen all kinds of people, rich and poor. All of them have an appointment with death. The rich fool in the parable of Jesus was enjoying the good life, building bigger barns, putting away food and drink so that his life would be a nonstop party for years. Then—like a clap of lightning—he was in the presence of his Maker. Like the rich fool, our lives will be required of us—maybe tonight. We cannot know. All we can be sure about is what we do with this very moment. So shouldn't our priorities be (1) to be sure of our own salvation and (2) to be sure of as many others' as possible?

I've completed number one and marked it off my list. I am in the grip of Jesus, and Satan himself can't do a thing about that. My life is devoted now to the second point. I want to stand at the gates of heaven with a delegation of people—the more the merrier—who are there by my invitation, directly or indirectly. I want to feel good about how I spent the time I had, not having stood with my hands in my pockets, but having busied myself in the rescue mission.

Statistically Urgent

Maybe theological terminology leaves you cold, but you like numbers and statistics. As I've mentioned, I've served with a task force to assess the readiness of the world for our efforts to fulfill the Great Commission. I've seen the numbers, and they're not pretty. Are you ready to do the math with me?

Theoretically, only God can see the state of a soul. He and only He can offer the true count of where His people are spiritually, but we can do a certain amount of research. We can get a good, broad idea of where we stand, using the best studies and scholarship available. I hope you'll visit the websites of effective missions organizations such as the International Mission Board. They can offer you much more detail on these findings.[1] They have the long answer, so I'm going to give you the condensed version.

At present, there are 7 billion passengers on Spaceship Earth. What percentage of those would you estimate to have heard the gospel? The task force has concluded that more than 750 million of those (that is, 75 percent of 1 billion) have heard and believed the gospel of Jesus Christ. This means 11 people of every 100 in this world are willing to claim Jesus as personal Lord and Savior. Keep in mind that a great number of people list "Christian" as their religious preference without truly knowing Christ in a personal way. (The figure of 33 percent is often given as the percentage of Christians in the world). The number of Spirit-filled, evangelical believers who are willing to lead others to Christ, of course, is nowhere close to the total number of people claiming to be followers of Jesus.

The number is better than the 0 percent we started out with, but the truth is that we have been given twenty centuries, and at present more than six billion people face the prospect of hell. This isn't, of course, to include the countless millions and billions who have died before we could reach them in those two thousand years.

More: About 38 percent of the world's population (that is, 2.6 billion) has heard the gospel and rejected it. At least they have received the message and had the opportunity, although we can't know how effectively and lovingly the gospel was presented to them. Just over 50 percent of the world's population (that is, 3.5 billion) has no realistic opportunity to hear the gospel at present. The number is increasing gradually. These are people we are not in position to reach because there are no believing Christians anywhere in their communities.[2]

Don't you want to hear about fervent, Spirit-filled, loving Christians going to live in all those communities, so that people can know God has loved them enough to send His one and only Son as a gift to them? I have an urgent desire to see that happen, and I'm following missions news every single day to read of any new developments in Africa, Asia, South America, or anywhere there are people who have had no exposure to the gospel.

Here is a challenging number: 11,646. That's the total number of people groups in the world. (There are 584 unreached people groups in the United States.) You may think of your globe in terms of countries, each one a uniform color. But within most of those countries are many distinct people groups, often with their own languages and values. The task forces of the International Mission Board of the Southern Baptist Convention have spent many years simply identifying the groups so that we can begin to figure out the best way to reach them. It's not going to be the same strategy for every single group.

Of these 11,646 people groups, 6,734 groups contain less than 2 percent evangelical Christians.[3] Many of them have no missionary activity targeting them, no churches being planted with them, no one so much as praying for them. Is that not a tragedy? We know God yearns to be reconciled with every single member of every single people group. Surely He is saying to us, *I have so many children—so many—that you don't even know, that you haven't even found. They are My lost sheep. Each one is precious to Me. I hear them crying out in confusion and pain, hungry physically and spiritually. Can't you find the time to rescue them?*

Let me assure you that all the news isn't depressing. For example, the fastest-growing religion in the world is Islam—in itself a very discouraging fact. But one particular segment of Christianity is growing faster. That segment is evangelical Christianity. Last year, two hundred thousand people in Saudi Arabia downloaded the Bible from the Internet.[4] We're reaching great numbers of women from within Islam because of the startling difference between what the New Testament offers them and what the Qur'an offers them. At present, prodemocracy movements in the Islamic Arab world, fueled by Facebook and other technologies, are opening windows for the gospel all the time. Think of the change in geopolitical tension if the Spirit of God began to move through the Middle East!

The global situation may be improving in some places, but what about here at home? The population of the United States at this writing is just over 308.7 million. You would expect the numbers to look much stronger in a nation with a Christian heritage, and you would be right. Even so, according to projections of the North American Missions Board, more than 233 million Americans (that is, 75 percent) do not have a saving relationship with Jesus Christ. Of the fifty-five million people in nine northeastern states, 83 percent have no saving relationship with Jesus Christ.[5] This includes the historic area where the Pilgrims brought their amazing faith to the New World, where Jonathan Edwards preached during the Great Awakening. Having been awakened, the greater part of this area has gone back to sleep.

The Christian majority that has often been imagined is a myth, if we use any biblical definition of *Christian*. And we're losing ground. Young people in their twenties are walking away from the Christian faith in far higher percentages than in any past generation. Right now, religions of all kinds are blossoming inside the borders of our country. Other faiths are sending missionaries to us.

Tom Clegg and Warren Bird wrote a book called *Lost in America*. They made the statement that the unchurched population in this country, if it were extracted and set down somewhere as a nation of its own, would be the fifth-largest nation in the world.[6] That would make the United States the world's third-largest mission field. Yes, we see churches on every corner, but how many are truly preaching the gospel? How many are equipping the saints to evangelize their friends and support world missions? Even among many of our more effective churches, how many believers can articulate the gospel well enough to share it? We can at least be intelligent in our strategies. We know that 83 percent of Americans live in metropolitan areas, so it makes sense to target our cities in a special way. LA, Chicago, NYC—name a big city, and you'll find a big need. I learned that within New York City, more than eight hundred languages are spoken.[7] It's a city of many nations!

Downtown, uptown, and out of town, the need is great. Across the oceans, the need is even greater. Spin the globe, close your eyes, and put your finger down on any section of populated land, and you'll be pointing to a place where people need the Lord. The numbers add up to urgency.

Strategically Urgent

Strategy is presented in the very marching orders Jesus gave us: "But you will receive power when the Holy Spirit has come upon you, and you will be My witnesses in Jerusalem, in all Judea and Samaria, and to the ends of the earth" (Acts 1:8). Do you see the progression? He starts with the place His listeners happen to be standing and moves progressively farther away. In each succeeding place, there are greater demographic differences with which to contend. Jesus highlights a regional, national, and international strategy for being His witnesses.

Interestingly enough, however, Jesus never uses the word *then*. He uses *and*, so the progress is geographical, not chronological. We will be His witnesses here in the city *and* in the country *and* in the next country *and* everywhere else. That presents a problem, doesn't it? We ask Jesus, "Where first, here or there?" and He answers, "Yes." We are left to struggle with how to allot our efforts. What are we doing for the Great Commission close to home? What are we doing across the sea?

Jesus offered the ultimate mission statement in Acts 1:8, and at Cross Church, we've absorbed it into our own missional vision: "Reaching Northwest Arkansas, America, and the world for Jesus Christ." That statement is our guide and our interpreter as we plan all we do as a church. We've discovered we can be about all kinds of good and worthy Great Commission business, as long as it fulfills that statement.

I believe in a personal and progressive vision for missions. I have to own Acts 1:8 personally. It is written in my soul that I must see the gospel taken to places and people where it has yet to penetrate. That requires a progressive, organized strategy. Therefore, I must be a citizen of the world. I know from my travels that when I have been among people, I can better love them and pray for them. So at the very least, I need to educate myself. I need to learn all I can about the many nations, the people groups, their needs, and how I can meet them. Every one of these groups must be reached in its own unique way.

We have one gospel but thousands of groups, billions of individuals. Jesus died for both Malawi and Minneapolis, but we must approach each of those in a different way as we bring the news of the gospel. We call this "contextualizing our strategy." In past centuries, missionaries went to Africa or China and forced the people there to sing Western hymns and wear Western clothing. Hopefully we're a lot smarter and more loving now. We know these people have a cultural context. We want to respect it and use it as a channel for sharing the love of Christ. When I think of the work entailed in mastering all these contexts, I personally feel the urgency yet again.

I believe that perhaps the most strategic solution to the challenge of the Great Commission lies in churches that do not yet exist. We need to be planting churches intelligently and aggressively—churches that are ready to address languages, cultures, and needs; churches in proportion to and in the style of the communities they encompass; churches with energetic leaders who are hungry to see a vast revival. In a typical American city, we need many thousands of new churches.

Have we begun to wrestle with the profound implication of that statement? We can't reach billions of people with our current means. Every existing church should now be planting multiple new churches.

Personally Urgent

Just as I own Acts 1:8, I must own the Great Commission personally. I must come to a place where it is unthinkable for me to leave the work to others, to hire it done. I should not be able to imagine this work as someone else's "problem." In Matthew 28 and Acts 1, I hear Jesus speaking to *me*—not to a group of eleven long-dead fishermen and peasants. I read the rest of Acts and see it as a case study for *me*—not a history of how ancient people traveled and had adventures. I read the stories of Hudson Taylor and William Carey and know they are my brothers, my predecessors, who are handing off the fruit of their labor to *me*—not colorful heroes from a devotional story.

The Great Commission is mine. It was made for me, and me for it. I can imagine life without it no more than I can imagine life without my head. I am responsible. I am accountable. I'll admit, I would feel pressure if it were only me. I would be bearing two thousand years of history, and all of eternity, on my slim shoulders; and that would be a bit much. But this is a burden I share with many other people. My church helps me carry it. My wife and family shoulder it with me. Brothers and sisters in Christ, known and unknown to me, have stepped up to be accountable with me. Together, we are going to own this thing.

In the Old Testament, Ezekiel was another prophet charged with warning the people of God's judgment. He felt that if he could simply be faithful in delivering the message, then the blood would not be on his hands if the people rejected it. He also reasoned that if he had the truth and failed to give it to them, then their blood would be on his hands (Ezekiel 3:18). Who could live with such a legacy? He developed a sense of urgency about spotless hands. He took responsibility for what he had and others needed.

At some point, the discussion of the Great Commission has to stop being about theology, mission philosophy, and the like; it must become personal. Like Old Testament prophets, we don't want the blood of others on our hands. But from a New Testament point of view, we want the joy of a heavenly rendez-vous with grateful, rescued souls. That desire, too, is personal with me. I have the opportunity to have an impact on eternity itself:

- Heaven is said to be perfect, yet I can make it even *better*.
- Heaven is said to be infinite, yet I can make it *larger*.
- Hell is a place I will never visit, but I can spend eternity enjoying the knowledge that I helped reduce its size.

What's on your calendar for today? Any agenda items more pressing than those?

Reaching a Flat World

Thomas L. Friedman dared to write what he called, in the subtitle, *A Brief History of the Twenty-First Century*. His 2005 book, *The World Is Flat*, was a runaway best seller that has quickly changed the paradigm for how business and culture work in this new millennium.[8]

How exactly is the world "flat"? Friedman uses the term in reference to the "even playing field" that he now sees in international commerce. In other words, those who held the high ground for so long—the big names that ruled business—may have lost many of their advantages.

It's a whole new world, and the "little guy" has an opportunity, if he will only see it. For example, Friedman recounts examples of companies in China and India that have provided call-center operators or labor. As a result of these, the idea of the global village is becoming a reality. Companies like Microsoft and AT&T have labor forces intertwined all across the globe. Geographical limitations are over.

He speaks of the fall of the Berlin Wall, which was more than symbolic; a true barrier battered into rubble. With the death of Russian communism, a toppled wall meant an open door. Shortly thereafter, the Internet quickly reached beyond all boundaries to create what was then called an "information superhighway" that theoretically linked everyone.

You hold a book in your hand—or is it an e-book?

Here, too, the playing field has been leveled. Anyone with computer access and an idea to share can quickly publish a book that is available anywhere and everywhere.

Friedman's point is that it's a new day for business. *My* point is that God is working out His purpose. Spend a lengthy period immersed in little but the Great Commission, as I have done, and you begin to see the patterns: our Lord is clearing the runway, removing obstacles, creating links, putting everything in place for His servants to carry the Great Commission to completion.

Meanwhile, as God does His part, we must be absolutely clear on our own task. The Great Commission is a concept that carries throughout Scripture, from the first chapter until the last. It is simply inherent in the story of the relationship between God and His children. The idea is phrased in several ways in the New Testament, the central expression being found in Matthew's gospel:

> Then Jesus came near and said to them, "All authority has been given to Me in heaven and on earth. Go, therefore, and make disciples of all nations, baptizing them in the name of the Father and of the Son and of the Holy Spirit, teaching them to observe everything I have commanded you. And remember, I am with you always, to the end of the age." (28:18–20)

Notice that the Great Commission has two anchors. On one end is the authority of Christ; on the other, the presence of Christ with us.

What more could anyone need? Going in the authority of the Lord of creation means that His full character and power stand behind us. If a strange man comes to your door at night and asks to come in, you would be a fool to let him do so. But if he showed you his credentials as a police officer, you would immediately open your door. It would no longer matter that you were looking at an unfamiliar face; his authority would speak for itself, powerful and trustworthy. When we go in the name of Jesus, we know that "all authority has been given to [Him] in heaven and earth." Infinite power stands behind us; the gates of hell shall not prevail against this mission.

We should add, however, that He doesn't simply stand behind us: He stands *beside* us: "Remember," He says, "I am with you always." There may be any number of tasks that might have frightened me in childhood, but I knew I could face them if a grown-up went with me. We are promised so many times in Scripture that our Lord will never leave us or forsake us. When we are going forward in obedience to His command, however, this is the time when we feel His presence most of all.

What would you guess is the most cited reason that people refuse to share their faith? You probably guessed it: *fear.* When I think about the vast number of Christians who are afraid to speak in His name, I can only conclude that they haven't read and understood Matthew 28:18–20, because Jesus has completely removed any reason for you or me to be afraid. He promises His power and authority; He promises to go with us.

What, then, is the task? Clearly, it is to tell everyone in the world about Jesus Christ and to make disciples of all the nations. Over the centuries, people have attempted to distort these simple marching orders, to paper over them, or simply to ignore them.

There are four verb clauses in the command: *Go, make*

disciples, baptize, and *teach*. Actually, "go" is more accurately translated, "as you go." The other three actions are predicated on our forward progress, which Jesus simply takes for granted—He knows His children will do as He commands. Ultimately, however, the structure of the sentence makes it clear that the controlling phrase is *make disciples*. Jesus is saying, "As you go, *make disciples*." How? By *baptizing* them and *teaching* them to observe all that Jesus has taught us.

When we take in these words, just as Jesus said them, there is an overwhelming sense of action—an unstoppable force of good news for all men and women, wherever the news may find them:

As you go (implying we're already gone);
make disciples (raise up soldiers);
baptizing them (professing to the world their
   allegiance to Christ); and
teaching them (equipping them for the world with
   the teachings of Christ);
so that immediately these, too, are going, making
   disciples, baptizing, and teaching.

It's a "rinse and repeat" cycle until the whole world knows, until the waters of the world are clotted with new believers, until there is no one left to tell. Then, of course, Christ Himself will come.

That's the Great Commission. You and I are enfolded in the power and the presence of Christ Himself, as we burst forth on our mission, of going and reaching and baptizing and teaching.

We look at the task and it seems immense, intense,

impossible. It takes one of the world's wise men, Thomas L. Friedman, to tell us that in fact, the doors have never been more open. Once the world was a vanishing horizon in every direction, yet now it is flat. Now the rules are being rewritten.

Now is the time for mobilization.

CHAPTER 4

Transform Our Families

Where does the time go? My marriage to Jeana is in its thirty-fifth year, and it's still growing, still evolving. We had a deep love for each other on our wedding day, but we could never have imagined the plans God had for us, and the way He would use our partnership.

We were married on the final day of 1976. Four months earlier, I had begun pastoring my first church while still a seminary student. This was in Cherokee, Texas, where the population was three hundred. Each weekend we would climb into the car and drive a little more than an hour to preach and minister before the next week of classroom studies began. This is a common part of seminary training: studying during the week, then driving out into the country for an apprenticeship ministry experience over the weekend.

The early years of our marriage were intertwined with serving churches and launching a ministry career. I was blessed with a fabulous asset in what I had to offer a congregation: Jeana had a music degree with a concentration in piano. To this day, I believe I got my first job because a pianist came in the bargain. Church personnel committees love two-for-one deals.

Whatever field you choose, your first job is an exciting moment. You are fully motivated, ready to prove yourself. I was highly committed to reaching people for Christ. Even then, the Great Commission was at the heart of my faith. I walked through neighborhoods, knocked on doors, and met people from diverse backgrounds. If there were three hundred souls, I was going to do my utmost to ensure that every one of them was claimed for God's kingdom.

As Jeana and I gave our youthful energy to that town, the church grew both spiritually and numerically. People came to Christ. And all this time, we were also newlyweds. Jeana and I built our family in the context of building churches, reaching people, and living in the energy of the Great Commission. My two passions in life were Christ's bride (the church) and my bride (Jeana). We didn't compartmentalize things but committed ourselves to each other and to Christ with the same energy. Our devotion to ministry deeply enhanced our marriage, and the love in our marriage lent power and credibility to our ministry.

After all these years, Jeana and I are still doing marriage, ministry, and family as one thing rather than three. We try to live holistically. And marriage was only the beginning.

Branching Out

Jeana and I began our parenting years with no illusions about having perfect children. As a matter of fact, we knew all the stereotypes of preachers' kids. Yet everything went right for us. In time, God gave us two wonderful sons, Josh and Nick. All through their teens, our sons lived for Christ and gave us, their parents, love and obedience rather than the typical friction that might be expected during those years. They poured themselves into church and group activities with the same devotion with which their parents poured themselves into ministry. Our two boys led friends to Christ. They cherished their mission trips and took active interest in all the ways our church reached out.

Now I enjoy the deep pleasure of watching our little family branch out and increase its impact. Josh is a high school football coach who is passionate about young men and their families. He has already won four state championships, but he feels the real victories have come in the hearts of many of his players. He and his wife, Kate, now have three sons of their own, Peyton, Parker, and Jack Bailey; and caring for small children hasn't caused them to miss a beat in ministering to the community and leading mission trips.

Nick makes his parents equally proud. He serves as campus pastor of Cross Church Fayetteville. He has earned bachelor's, master's, and doctoral degrees and developed his own unique prophetic voice—he's a true twenty-first-century communicator of God's Word. He and his wife, Meredith, have two children, and as I write, they're working to adopt twins from Ethiopia. Why? They are citizens of the world; they take the Great Commission personally. Reaching the nations is their reason for building their family.

God deserves all the credit and glory for the way things have turned out with our family. Jeana and I always did our best, but we know that's not always enough. Parenting is one of life's greatest challenges, and it can go in many directions, even for the best of parents. God has woven our family and our ministry together in such an intricate fashion, each strengthening the other. It's clear that this is the way God designed life to work—husband, wife, and children bonded as only a family can be; focused on the right things as only a family following Christ can be; then sending the children out to multiply our impact.

Even so, I know many committed, Jesus-following couples who have made all the right moves as parents, trusted everything to God, but still had heartaches in parenting. Who could say why? We do our best to raise our children biblically, but our kids still have free wills. The enemy opposes our efforts, and the world is filled with lures and snares. I counsel parents who are despondent over the choices their children—even adult children—have made. I try to remind them that God is the perfect parent, yet even He has problem children.

When it all works according to plan, however, what a beautiful result. I can remember that young couple napping on the pews at the little church in Cherokee, Texas—so young, so tired from driving back and forth, balancing seminary and ministry and marriage. Now that young couple has seven grandchildren and a legacy of ministry. Who could have foreseen it?

It goes fast too. It seems as if, only a few months ago, Jeana and I were walking up and down the avenues of Cherokee, knocking on doors, telling people about Jesus, and inviting them to church. That was Great Commission for Beginners. In the parable of the talents (Matthew 25:14–30), the master tests his servants with the smaller things; then he entrusts them with the larger ones. After all these years, we have godly children and grandchildren to extend our reach. We have strategies and the opportunities through our church and denomination, through media and the Internet. We are finding new strategies and focusing on new areas of the Great Commission—orphans, for example.

If God wants us to put on our jackets and walk up and down the street again, we're ready. Whatever He wants, that's what we want. Obeying the Great Commission may begin simply, it may begin as a responsibility, but it always becomes a deep passion, a matter of the heart. We can't imagine any other way of life. We want the family of Floyd to help reach the family of mankind.

That approach is a part of our last great hope in this world. We cannot transform the world unless we first transform our families. We need to be raising our children to love people of all kinds, from those on the street to those on the other side of the world. We want our kids to have hearts for their communities and for other nations, as well as a passion for everyone on this planet to hear the gospel and be discipled as believers. Yes, it's a daunting challenge, but it's our challenge. The harder the task, the more glory for God. So let's get started transforming our families. In this chapter, I'm going to be very practical about how to do it.

The Heart of Parenting

The people of Israel had a mentor named Moses, and he offered them a powerful basis for family building:

> Love the LORD your God with all your heart, with all your soul, and with all your strength. These words that I am giv-ing you today are to be in your heart. Repeat them to your children. Talk about them when you sit in your house and when you walk along the road, when you lie down and when you get up. (Deuteronomy 6:5–7)

Deuteronomy 6 is the nonnegotiable, essential, lowest com-mon denominator of all parenting. If raising kids were a game (it's not, of course), Deuteronomy 6 would be square one.

On trips to Israel, our Israeli guide, Avi, always tells our group,

"You Americans read the Bible too fast. Slow down. Read it slowly." He has a point. To read the Bible "too fast" is like getting the greatest feast of your life from a drive-through window, then wolfing it down without even thinking about it. Every detail of Scripture is a world of teaching in itself. Context is everything.

We're going to read Deuteronomy 6 one more time, this time in slow motion. I predict you'll see ideas that you've never noticed there before.

Let Parents Be Disciples

Yes, we all know the importance of discipling our children. We focus so much on the idea that we forget what is back on square one. "These words that I am giving you today," Moses says, "are to be in *your* heart" (Deuteronomy 6:6; emphasis added). Moses starts with the parents' hearts. We are the ones who are to love the Lord with all that is in us. Everything else proceeds from that premise. We are to devote ourselves wholeheartedly to God, or the rest is simply bound to fail. There are parents who faithfully drop their children off at Sunday school every week, then go home to read the funnies. It almost doesn't matter how wonderful the Sunday school teachers are; if the children don't see the love of God in their own parents, their faith will not take root.

We have to define our very lives in terms of discipleship. There's no way to fake it—not within the walls of our own homes. If someone were to ask our children to describe their parents, we would want their first response to be, "They are devout followers of Jesus Christ." Years from now, after we are gone, our children's enduring images should come from noticing us in prayer, in Bible study, in ministry. They should remember those things, and particularly our joy in doing them. If we are passionate Christ-followers, that in itself will cover a multitude of mistakes. We can afford to get a few other things wrong. If we are not strong disciples, then we can do all the other right things, and they won't make much of a difference. Our children won't hear a word we say while our actions are speaking at a higher volume.

The example you set is your child's first gospel. Your actions, your reactions, your emotions, your values, and everything in you should tell a consistent story of walking in Christ. If your children believe what they see, they will read the true Bible. They will begin to follow its Author. Love God with all your heart, soul, and strength. It's the most important parenting skill of them all.

Let Parents Make Disciples

Having begun to demonstrate with our lives how to walk with God, we can begin to teach with our mouths what it means to be a believer. The instruction of Moses is for us to be consistent about that teaching:

> Talk about [these truths] when you sit in your house and when you walk along the road, when you lie down and when you get up. (Deuteronomy 6:7)

He counsels us to *repeat* the teaching; repetition is a powerful teaching tool. Repetition is a powerful teaching tool. (See what I mean?) Discuss the law of God as you go and stay, as you rise and sleep, or to say it more succinctly, *always*.

In a family, every moment is a teachable moment. Every decision is a commentary on the influence of faith. That happens regardless of intent, right? Even when we don't realize it, we are broadcasting messages to our watching children 24/7. We might be teaching a child how to shoot a basketball or how to do a math problem, how to set a table, how to drive a car, or how to treat the opposite sex. There is the surface subject, and beneath it is a layer of godly influence. For example, you twist an ankle under the basket while teaching the jump shot. The maturity with which you handle that moment, as a disciple of Jesus, teaches your child on a different level than the mechanics of basketball. Your patience, your enjoyment of playing together, and even the time you offer to your child—these all reflect something about God, because you have identified yourself with God. You are the child's model of what it means to believe in and serve God.

There is a common saying that I like, though I have no idea who originated it: "Parents teach what we know, but reproduce what we are." Stop and think about that; it's a serious and humbling thought. Children learn with their minds what we say. They learn with their hearts what we show. Every parent has had that sad moment when he sees in a child something he never intended to pass on to him. I have habits and tendencies, some good, some not. I would love to sift through them carefully and choose which ones my children can have, but life doesn't work that way. I wish I weren't impatient, and I feel worse about my own impatience when I see it in either of my sons. I knew early on that I wanted my children to miss out on inheriting this trait. I could emphasize it when discussing character, but a far more effective way to encourage them to be patient is by being patient myself.

Thus, by word and by deed, we want to build young disciples in our homes. Let's discuss the process of doing that.

Evangelize Your Children

I know all parents want assurance of their children's salvation. Maybe they'll give their lives to Christ at church. Maybe they'll go to some kind of Christian camp or youth function and respond to an invitation there. But we don't want to leave it to chance and to other personalities. We want to evangelize our own children.

One of the reasons people lack confidence in sharing their faith—even with their own children—is that they convince themselves they need a full seminary education and an encyclopedic knowledge of the Scriptures before they can open their mouths. The enemy would love for us to believe that, because then nobody would share his or her faith.

Know the basics. Understand what sin is—the disobedience that separates us from God—and how every single one of us is born in sin. Since God is perfect, we cannot spend eternity with Him while our natures are blackened by our sinfulness. Yet God loves us so much that He found a way for us to come home to Him. He sent His Son, who lived a perfect life yet took the punishment we had earned, so that we can enjoy the reward that was rightfully His. Jesus rose from the dead so that we can live forever as well. Can you master this paragraph? Can you make it come to life as you talk about its ideas?

The most powerful witness is a personal one. Talk about your own journey of faith. There are always three parts to that: (1) your life before Christ, (2) how you came to accept Christ, and (3) how your life has been different ever since. Your children are already interested in what you were like when you were younger. Find opportunities to show them the difference Christ has made for you.

As you offer God's plan for salvation, help your children understand that they simply have to realize their sinfulness, ask God to forgive it through His Son, and accept the gift of salvation, asking Him to be Lord and Master from now on. Assure them that once they've said yes to Jesus, He will come to live in their hearts and they will begin to grow to be more like Him, a little more each day. Nothing is more wonderful and more joyful than knowing God! Life will still have its problems, but Jesus has promised to be with us and to help us in all things.

At the right time, when you feel the prompting of the Holy Spirit, explain these things in a quiet place. Make sure your child has a basic understanding of them, and trust God to do the rest. Pray together, allowing your child to verbalize his or her understanding of sin and desire to be forgiven in Christ. Make it a celebration: write down the date and the location where your child first received Christ. This is a spiritual birthday to commemorate! Later, they're going to have the memory of where they were, but it will be nice for them to also know the date. Memorialize it. Remember the anniversary each year.

You'll also want to get your pastor or children's minister involved. A minister will listen carefully and affirm that your child understands what has come to pass and has truly become a disciple of Jesus Christ. The next step is usually baptism, a beautiful symbol of the way Christ purifies us from sin and raises us to walk in newness of life. It's also a joyful statement to the world: "I have decided to follow Jesus!"

Baptism should always come as soon after the salvation experience as possible. It's so important to be intentional about leading your children to Christ, from the explanation to the acceptance to the prayer to the baptism. These things will help your children understand the reality of the things that have happened within them. They will always know, *I am a Jesus-follower. I began following Him on this date. I was baptized on this other date.*

Salvation is a foundation on which to build a life, and your shovel will begin the digging to set the cornerstone in place.

Expect Your Children to Grow as Disciples

When my boys were just beginning to read, I taught them what it means to spend time with God each day. They knew that this was something I did, and as young boys, of course, they were eager to walk in their daddy's footsteps—another reason we need to evangelize our children before adolescence, when so many complicating factors kick in.

My sons were proud of their time with God, and they loved discussing it with me. They were young, but I didn't worry that they would find the time empty. I expected them to grow as disciples and to approach Jesus as the King of kings and Lord of lords, not just as a casual friend. I stressed that as wonderful as He is, He wants to be with them for a special period every single day. What a privilege! That is better than having the president of the United States wanting to spend time with them. Better than a movie star or pro athlete. I did my best to spark their young spirits, and I left the rest to the Spirit of God, who has a perfect knowledge of how to speak to children.

It's tragic that parents sometimes let the matter of faith drift into oblivion as soon as their children have been baptized. I've never understood that way of thinking, but I suppose it's part of casual Christianity: "My child is a member of the church, so we can check off religion. Now we need to see about ballet lessons or Little League." We need to be intentional about beginning the discipleship process with our children, or it won't be long before their conversion experiences are just vague and meaningless memories.

God speaks to children in a way that is perfectly suited to them. Jesus, we observe, was adored by little ones—it was the disciples who tried to shoo them away, assuming that children just wouldn't understand. We need to expect and trust Him to whisper into our children's souls, rather than anticipating boredom on their parts. The Holy Spirit will come to live within them. He will make a start on His wonderful transformational work during the wonder years, when the mind is young and flexible and so much is possible.

Let's set the standard where God would have us set it, and expect our children to begin following Jesus at no more or less than the level appropriate to their ages.

Engage Your Children in the Life of the Church

I hope and pray your family is immersed in a lively, Bible-believing, ministry-driven, Great Commission church. There is every reason to do that, of course, but children loom large in that decision. We live in an age of fabulous, effective children's ministry in the churches that are paying attention. So many guests make second visits to our church simply because their kids loved their experience and begged their parents to bring them back.

The church will provide wonderful assistance through its ministries to children and youth. It will help you teach the Bible, share a love of missions, and lay all the groundwork for a life of being engaged in local church ministry. If you have teenagers, take a long, hard look at the youth ministry. Does it have small groups for Bible study? Does it send its youth on trips for mission and ministry, locally and internationally? Sit down with the youth minister, build a relationship, and offer your time and support even as you're sharing your expectations.

A good measure of a biblical church is this: it doesn't simply provide programs for activity consumers; it sets requirements for families to show their faithfulness. The right church will challenge your family to move forward as disciples and as Great Commission believers. It will ask something of you, rather than simply provide fun and fellowship. It will be a Jesus-centered church, and its heart will be winning nonbelievers to the gospel, then making disciples.

Help your children understand that Sunday is God's special day. When many of us were coming of age, respect for the sanctity of the Sabbath was almost a given. Few secular organizations held any meetings on that day, and restaurants and stores were often closed. Today, however, your children will tell you they have soccer practices or Girl Scout trips on Sundays. God enshrined the Sabbath when He created the world, and again when He gave the Ten Commandments. It is a holy day. Your children will watch to see how you, as parents, align your family's priorities. If the church loses out whenever its functions conflict with some other event, then the message will be clear: other things are more important than God's things. Jesus didn't teach casual discipleship. He taught that it had a cost, that it required painful decisions, and that at times we need to walk away from other things we might have intended to do. This is why we recognize that every moment is a teachable moment. Even when you don't realize it, you'll be teaching decisions and values and priorities all the time, and your children will take in every bit of it. From the outset, it's so important that we make a covenant to place Christ at the head of our family and the church above other activities.

I have yet to see a young person who is a passionate follower of Christ without being actively engaged in a local church. Get your kids involved, even when that means making sacrifices. You'll willingly make those sacrifices when you realize the difference a good church makes in the life of your child.

Equip Your Children to Go to the Nations

From the beginning, talk to your children about a world full of lost people. Establish in their minds that Jesus Christ is the only answer for people who are lost. And as you teach them the Lord's Prayer, Psalm 23, David and Goliath, Noah and the ark, and other favorite passages, put the Great Commission at the forefront.

Children like adventure. Teenagers are stirred by grand visions. Help them see that going to all the nations in the name of Christ is the great adventure and grand vision of life. Nothing is more exciting, more challenging, or more wonderful in conception. Educate them about the diverse people groups of each continent. Post a world map somewhere in your home, and talk about the many fascinating places in the world, and the need for people to know Christ in every country. Collect the inspiring stories of contemporary people who are going to the nations, offering themselves for furthering the Great Commission.

Consider your efforts an investment to pay dividends down the road. When the time comes for your growing children to begin thinking about careers, you will have planted many seeds within them and given those seeds time to take root. You'll be proud to have children of the world who have a passion for seeing the nations come to Christ. There are many possible careers that fit into a Great Commission life, here or abroad. And whatever direction they choose—doctor, lawyer, sales, finance—that career can be a Great Commission career.

I've actually seen parents do the opposite. God calls their children to missions, and they stand in the way of their kids accepting the call because they don't like the possibility of their children traveling to some distant—and possibly dangerous—place. As Jesus said, "Don't try to keep them from coming to Me" (Matthew 19:14).

Neither should we try to keep them from going for Him. What a tragic mistake, to stand in opposition to a selfless, God-centered decision on the parts of our kids. I'm thankful God gave up His own Son to come to the most dangerous place possible out of love for us. Knowing what has been done for me, how could I do any differently?

We have the opportunity to cooperate with the Lord in preparing the next generation to take the gospel to the world, if we don't complete our task in this generation. The Internet has already changed the equation for us—who knows how much more of a global village we will be in a decade or two, if Christ hasn't returned? Each day draws us closer to fulfilling what has been laid out for us and closer to preparing the world for His triumphant reentry.

The Shiloh Story

Shiloh Christian School is a ministry of our church, with K–12 grade levels. Hundreds of families trust our church to come alongside them to help disciple their children, and we believe that's the highest compliment those families could pay us. We will do whatever it takes to serve them well in helping to train their children.

Shiloh was the result of a vision from God. I could see our church placing high school students all around the world, pursuing mission endeavors before their graduation. Through the generous giving of Commission-minded supporters, we are able to pay for the first trip. After that experience, giving them the initial taste of serving God in missions, they pay their own way—and many of them are more than willing to do so.

It is my passion to see swelling numbers of high school students involved in worldwide missions outside the United

States even while they are young. These are the years when their adult worldviews will be formed, the times when they are most impressionable. We have an incredible opportunity to impact the world by changing high school students. I want our teens to (1) have a true, biblical worldview; (2) see people who are hungry for the gospel firsthand; and (3) have a powerful experience that will play a part when they decide their future careers.

I cannot express in writing the strong emotions I feel as I think about our students all across the world, and as I see them come home with tears in their eyes and a new passion in their hearts, eager to tell parents and siblings and teachers and coaches and friends all about how they found the meaning of being used by God while working somewhere far away. I love going to the airport and seeing them step off the planes with that glow on their faces. Then I squint my eyes a bit, and I imagine these fresh-faced young people just a little older, marrying and beginning families of their own. Think of it: Their children will be second-generation Great Commission people. They will never know any other way of life than one focused on sharing the news of Jesus Christ with the world. Some of them will become traditional overseas or domestic missionaries. Others will pursue what some unimaginatively consider "secular" careers. You and I will know the truth: there is no truly secular career for someone who loves Jesus. These businesspeople, engineers, technology workers, lawyers, medical personnel, and homemakers will be Great Commission workers just as much as those who have gone to Brazil or Laos or Uganda.

They'll understand that there is always something we can do, wherever we are, whatever we are, to be obedient to the command of Jesus. I have a church filled with people who live in Northwest Arkansas, do every kind of job, and have a worldwide impact in many different ways.

Elevate the Great Commission to Job One

Finally, we need to create a mind-set that keeps the Great Commission first in our hearts and minds, the guiding principle of all that we do. Let me suggest some ways to do this.

Pray for the Great Commission

Communing with God and bringing Him our requests is always the starting point. Families need to be praying together every day. They can pray for missionaries by name; they can pray for countries and crises. Whatever is happening in the world's hot spots, families can ask God's glory to be served in some way, so that in time we begin to think of world events as fitting God's ultimate plan, though we don't know how. Families can keep informed in their churches' Great Commission involvements and pray every day for those ties. They can take advantage of special mission weeks and prayer weeks in their denominations. They can give offerings and pray for them. Prayer should never be underestimated. God is still listening, and our prayers are the fulcrum for all He is going to do through us.

Practice the Great Commission

Next we can roll up our sleeves and get involved. There are ways to speak the name of Jesus and minister in His name across the street, across town, across cultures and languages, and across the oceans. We need to remember that those in our families, our schools, and our communities are part of the Great Commission. We can begin with them, though we should never stop with them.

I love finding ways to enable families to serve together sharing the gospel of Christ. For example, in Cross Church's annual Thanksgiving Blessing Basket ministry, family groups offer their entire day to ministry, service, and evangelism of thousands of needy families. This blesses God, but every family will tell you they reap just as great a blessing. They give thanks every bit as much as the needy people they have helped, because they have been changed as mothers, fathers, sisters, brothers, children, or grandparents. They have a family memory they will cherish and an experience to build on.

There are so many ways your family can pursue the Great Commission. Why not take a mission trip together? Even if the whole family can't go, send some of you. No travel experience is more satisfying.

Give to the Great Commission

I believe in giving back to God, through the local church, the first tenth of all He has given our family. I also believe in special missions giving above and beyond that tithe. Why wait until there is a call for a missions offering and decide then whether you can afford it? I recommend putting missions giving into your family budget. Save for it, and make this a big point in your discussions. You'll be surprised at how your children will freely give of their allowances and savings when their hearts have been touched by need. Set the pace for your family. Give sacrificially. Support mission work across the globe, and discuss the results in family meetings.

Many churches emphasize missions at Christmas. Of course, that's the time when we spend the most money on gifts for each other. So many of our gifts are things we don't really need, so turn the tables and have a Great Commission Christmas. I've known families who give more to international missions than they choose to spend on one another during the season. Other people make it known that they don't need any new clothing or gadgets, but they would cherish a missions gift given in their names.

Giving, of course, is a matter to work out with God as you pray and then as you talk as a family. Give as you feel led, but realize that the Bible teaches that giving is an important discipline, and God blesses it in wonderful ways—among them the feeling of joy that sacrifice gives you. God always gives something back.

Adopt and Care for Orphans

Not long ago, I began to feel a deep conviction about the orphan crisis in our world. According to UNICEF, as of 2009 there were 163 million orphans across the globe. We can't even begin to imagine that many children without parents. It's a pandemic problem.

The heart of the gospel is the doctrine of adoption. The Bible tells us that there was a time when we ourselves were orphans, separated from our heavenly Father, hopeless and lost. Yet through Jesus, we have been adopted into the family of God. We have the privilege of becoming heirs to the kingdom. How, then, can we not be moved by the plight of so many orphans? Surely we won't live in forgetfulness of how much gratitude we should have and express through godly service.

Matt Carter, lead pastor of the Austin Stone Church in Austin, Texas, says our greatest barrier to fulfilling the Great Commission is that 163 million children will have no understanding of what it means to be loved unconditionally by a parent. If they haven't seen a visible father who knows how to love them, how will they have faith in the One they can't see?[1] That's a profound thought. If we truly care about the Great Commission, then we must be serious about orphans. After all, the Bible speaks of our responsibility toward them throughout the Old and New Testaments.

What if Christian families everywhere began to reach out

to ease the orphan pandemic? They could adopt, of course, but even financial gifts could make a dramatic impact. They could help promote the cause, encouraging people in their small groups and Bible classes to join them in fighting the problem.

Mark Richt, head football coach at the University of Georgia, heard about the orphan crisis in his small group Bible study while he was still an assistant at Florida State. He and his wife decided to adopt a child from Ukraine. When they traveled there, they ended up adopting a second child as well—one with a facial birth defect—because they clearly felt God put it on their hearts to do so. For a long time, the Richts would not share their experience with the world, because Jesus teaches that we should do our good deeds secretly. But in time, they decided they wanted to get the word out and encourage adoption for others. Soon after that, Richt was offered the job at Georgia and given a much larger stage for his story. ESPN aired a special documentary on the story, and it traveled across the YouTube galaxy as well, touching hearts and encouraging people to consider adoption.[2]

Imagine millions of orphans being adopted by Christian families, raised in love, then allowed to participate in the spread of the gospel themselves. Many of them would return to their home countries, where they would share the gospel with others. This is no less than a blueprint for transforming the world.

As I mentioned earlier, my son and daughter-in-law have been led by God to adopt twins from Ethiopia, and I'm delighted to see them setting a standard for their generation. I do believe that young couples today will be far less selfish and far more world-minded if they open their homes, get involved in mission trips, and start fulfilling the Great Commission. I feel a deep sense of conviction about the selfishness of my own generation—the way we pleaded ignorance of this problem, the way we focused on our own homes and comfort while there was so much need. I've asked God's forgiveness for my own heart during those years, and I've determined that I will have an orphan focus as a component of my Great Commission vision for the rest of my days.

Zach and Erin Kennedy are another couple who have adopted from Ethiopia—in their case, a son. They already had three children of their own, and they could have said, "Our hands are full. We want to give our love to the kids we have." But instead, they listened to the Scriptures and the promptings of the Holy Spirit. Zach told us that one day he saw an empty place in the family van. There was room for one more child. The thought pierced his spirit: *How can we not adopt this little boy from Ethiopia?* They did, and like the Richts, one wasn't enough. They're in the process of adopting another orphan. It's interesting what happens when we obey God. Instead of it becoming a burden, His work is such a joy that we seek more service.

There's a lot of talk about a world sinking fast, and for good reason. But young couples such as Zach and Erin give me hope. In the hearts of our young people, a new compassion is blossoming. They are ready and eager to serve God in the world, to the point of bringing orphans into their homes. When I see this trend, I realize that with all the problems of our times, God is still in control. He has His plan, and I want to do everything I can to cooperate in it with Him.

Cross Church is also partnering with Esther's House Orphanage in Malawi, Africa. It's just one more way to do something. We can send aid and encouragement to those who live in the heart of the crisis, who take in orphans and people in need. There is no shortage of ways your church can plug in and fight for the future God wants.

In this and so many other ways, we can't just do business as usual with our families. The time has passed for that, although it should never have been. All along, we have been responsible to raise up Great Commission families; to say, "As for me and my family, we will worship the Lord," and then serve Him in the thing that is most precious to His heart (Joshua 24:15). He is a God who ordained the family from the very beginning. In the bond of love that a family has, we can begin to get just an inkling of the incredible, unconditional love of an adopting God. That love reaches toward a lost, dying world, and it won't allow us to focus on ourselves while so much needs to be done.

The Great Commission is awakening within families, changing them forever, giving them a future and a hope, a grand adventure to partake of forever. I challenge you to let this happen within your family.

CHAPTER 5

Capture Our
Communities

Travel transforms. New vistas expand our minds, showing us the world beyond our everyday boundaries. When I visit a place I've never been, I feel there's something new about me by the time I leave.

Even so, I came to a place in life where I felt the world held no more dramatic surprises for me. Then came a journey that turned me inside out and upside down. You might say the world rocked my world. In this journey, I didn't travel very far in miles—yet it took me twelve months to reach my destination. And one person changed me during that time, more so than any individual has ever changed me in my life.

The journey was actually my assignment by the Southern Baptist Convention to study the idea of a Great Commission resurgence. In the first chapter of this book, I described what it meant to me to work with a highly respected cast of Christian leaders and mission thinkers during 2009 and 2010, when the study took place. It was a journey to a new way of thinking, rather than to any particular location; and it was Jesus who spoke so profoundly to me, changing the way I see myself and my task forever.

Members of the task force worked hard together. It was a rigorous, pressurized year of study and thought before we brought our report and recommendations to the 2010 Southern Baptist Convention annual meeting. We were given two hours of presentation and discussion to summarize a year's worth of exploration. The conventional wisdom was that our recommendations would never pass. Many people are suspicious of any great level of change. Yet our recommendations were approved by a three-to-one margin of representatives from churches across the nation and world. Only history will prove the wisdom or folly of our conclusions. But here's the large point: we're talking about the Great Commission again. Our denomination has shifted on its great axis and is positioning itself, arming itself, and strategizing to reach the world for Christ and make disciples of all nations.

Since my earliest days of preaching, I'd felt I knew what it meant to have a heart for the Great Commission. All the churches I've pastored have placed evangelism and missions as the highest priority. But now, with a year to focus fully on the greatest desire of our Savior, what had been a glowing ember within me was kindled into a consuming flame. I was radically transformed, freshly recharged, and given a new lens for viewing an old mandate. I saw Jesus step into that brighter light and reveal Himself to me in a new way. I heard Him more clearly and felt His heart more powerfully. Now my way is clear: I must follow in obedience in all He wants me to do. The rest of my life belongs to Him and to the fulfillment of the Great Commission. The difference is one of the magnitude of my passion and the urgency of my desire.

I expect He will continue to reveal more to me as I need to

know it. I don't have a detailed map of the future; this is a journey of walking by faith. I do know what I've learned up to this point, and I know that what I see is new to me—or at least that I see it in new ways.

Land of the Lost

I think about a catchphrase from the movie *The Sixth Sense* in which a boy reveals he has seen ghosts. He says, "I see dead people." When asked how often, he replies, "All the time." Me too. I'm seeing it as never before—America, one more land of the lost. I look at our cities—and as I've told you, I love cities—and see darkness and death in the lively light. I look at my corner of the land, Northwest Arkansas, and see that here, too, is a region of lost people, regardless of the churches per capita. It's as if Christ has fitted me with new contact lenses. *Lord, how could I have been so blind? Why haven't I seen it the way I see it today?*

I see dead people. All the time.

But my mind has also changed. I think differently now. I have different ideas about what it means to be lost, about what it means to be a diverse nation and a diverse world. I think constantly about the need to know and to love and to understand all the people groups out there, so we can bring them the good news. I obsess over it, to be honest. I always knew that countless souls were heading for an eternity of punishment, but now I feel what that means. I think about it, visualize it, grieve over it. God doesn't desire that anyone should perish, and I think I'm drawing closer to His heart on that matter.

Thinking of these things reorders my day. I ask, "What would Jesus want me to do on this day? How, exactly, would He want me to do it? What busywork do I need to push out of the way so I can attend to what registers on the scale of eternity?"

And I really want the answer! It's an urgent craving to expend my time and energy significantly. *Here I am, Lord; send me!*

I'm still a local church pastor. Leading my church, leading my family, and organizing my personal life are all components of my central mission. I have made a covenant to lead a Great Commission church, a Great Commission family, and to have a Great Commission personal life. There are no cubicles, no dividing walls in the schematics of my thinking. So I expect my church, my family, and my private world to benefit from the time I've had with Jesus. That's how it always is with Jesus: win-win. Still, the deepest prayers I pray are for the gospel to be presented in places where it hasn't yet penetrated.

Everything changed for me during that journey with Jesus over one year. You might say I finally began to take hold of that for which Christ has taken hold of me, to put it in a Philippians 3:12 kind of way. This was the year in which He took hold of me in something like a headlock! His grip on my priorities is powerful, and I hope He never lets me go. My eyes are clear now, my brainwaves are bouncing, and the world is a very different place. I've since found out that I'm in good company. Consider, for example, that experienced world traveler named Paul.

It Begins with What You See

Imagine you're walking down the road of ancient Greece with Paul of Tarsus: tentmaker, itinerant evangelist, and church planter. The Mediterranean weather is lovely; the road, well built by the Romans, is dotted with travelers and peddlers from many nations. There are amazing conversations taking place as people walk. In time, your group realizes it is approaching Athens. Everyone becomes quiet as they enter the city. This is the intellectual center of the known world, the culture that has overwhelmed all other cultures. Even the Romans derive their gods and their philosophies from the Greeks.

If you are the type who loves a lively debate, you've come to the right place. All the great stand-up philosophers hang out downtown. New ideas flow like wine down the broad avenues of the metropolis. Religion? There's plenty of that, too, paganism being the hottest commodity. Shrines and temples dominate the streets, and most of them have been built for pagan gods.

But if you've been caught up in the new movement known as "the Way," or "Christianity," Athens is an intimidating place—maybe even a frightening one. The most learned men in the world are capable of pouncing on your every word, tying your logic into knots as everyone laughs.

Paul smiles with confidence. He's a Christian, and he loves a debate. He's ready to take on all opponents. As he enters town, he proceeds directly to the Aeropagus, a public court of philosophical opinion. Engaging the debaters here is like stepping on stage to challenge Eric Clapton to a guitar duel, halfway through your chord lessons. Yet Paul still wears his smile. The Bible picks up the story:

> Then Paul stood in the middle of the Areopagus and said: "Men of Athens! I see that you are extremely religious in every respect. For as I was passing through and observing the objects of your worship, I even found an altar on which was inscribed: TO AN UNKNOWN GOD. Therefore, what you worship in ignorance, this I proclaim to you." (Acts 17:22–23)

Paul knows the pundits of Athens take themselves very seriously. They figure they've cataloged all the various gods of the universe. Each one has its own shiny monument, and just for good measure, the Greeks have put up a catch-all plaque for "the unknown god," in case they've missed one.

Paul, a stranger to them, walks into their midst and builds a bridge by paying his respects. He commends them as connoisseurs of religion who are "extremely religious." Then he drops the bombshell. He tells them he has the scoop on the unknown god they've been worshipping in vague homage. This miscellaneous God is the only God, the one who made everything, and Athens doesn't have a temple that can hold Him. You can imagine the silence. The rustling of raised eyebrows; somewhere, a dog barks.

Ordinary travelers would have an eyeful of the masterpiece that is Athens. They would admire the monuments, the world-class architecture, and the imposingly learned academicians who preside over it all. Most people would see a thriving cityscape, filled with life. Paul looks around him and sees death. They would see a virtual theme park of gods. Paul sees the utter absence of God. He sees a lost world, never mind its art or its learning or its reputation. He sees what Jesus called "whitewashed tombs" (Matthew 23:27), sparkling on the outside and black with death and decay on the inside.

Paul honors the diversity of cultures. He says, "From one man He has made every nation of men to live all over the earth and has determined their appointed times and the boundaries of where they live" (Acts 17:26).

His point: many cultures don't need many gods. Only one could create the world and its people. Only one is Truth and Power. Greece had gods made in man's image; Paul speaks of men made in God's image.

As Paul grabs their attention and begins his address, he starts with the Greeks right where they stand. He makes use of their accustomed ideas and their visual props, their monuments. But he moves the debate from their home turf to God's.

He moves toward truth, revealing who God really is and why He requires repentance. He begins to speak of the resurrection of the dead, and he draws his first ridicule from some in the crowd. But he also begins to win new believers.

How we approach a situation depends upon what we see. Paul sees what they see—their people, their culture, their ideas, their impressive achievements—but at the same time, through the eyes of the Spirit, he sees people who are God's beloved children but have wandered away, have become entangled in their own sin, and will face punishment for that sin. Paul also sees the urgency of a rescue attempt. That's why he's willing to risk his life, unconcerned about ridicule. God's powerful, convicting Spirit is speaking through him. Paul needs only to be faithful, make his stand, open his mouth, and let God give the words.

The unknown God, Paul says, is no longer unknown. He has taken on human flesh and walked among us, so that we could see and hear and touch the God of the universe. So that we would know how much He loves us, that our sin debt could be paid, and that death is vanquished. Who would rather have an unknown God, when the known one is so breathtakingly wonderful, beyond anything humans could have ever conceived?

Eyes of Compassion

No wonder some of the Greeks heard and believed right on the spot. No wonder they dropped their many years of misguided philosophy to follow Jesus. The Bible tells us that even as some hooted in derision, a few said, "We will hear you about this again" (Acts 17:32). They felt the tug of the Spirit at their hearts. When Paul departed, some of them followed him. Luke, the author of Acts, gives names of these first Christians in Athens (17:34).

For this to happen, Paul had to get past what he could see on the human level. He had to stop being a tourist in this world and begin looking with the eyes of Jesus Christ. The Gospels often mention what Jesus saw. For example, Matthew wrote, "When He saw the crowds, He felt compassion for them, because they were weary and worn out, like sheep without a shepherd" (9:36).

Repeatedly the word *compassion* recurs; Jesus looks at lost people as aimless as sheep disconnected from the herd, and He is moved by their spiritual condition. The disciples, like anxious tourists, tended to look at the same people and see problems, headaches, and obstacles in the way of whatever city was on the itinerary. But Jesus sees with the eyes of the soul, and that determines how He interacts with people.

Do we have that vision? Can we look upon people who bow before other gods and see that what they truly need, what they *must* have, is Jesus? Are we willing to say it aloud, even if it brings a few hoots of derision from the crowd? After all, people today don't like to hear that "there is salvation in no one else, for there is no other name under heaven given to people by which we must be saved" (Acts 4:12). Nor do they want to hear what Jesus Himself said: "No one comes to the Father except through Me" (John 14:6). But what if it's the truth? The Bible, of course, proclaims from cover to cover that it is. Therefore we should see everything and everyone in this light. One question and only one question matters: "Who do people say that the Son of Man is?" (Matthew 16:13).

Often the problem is that we feel intimidated, just as Paul might have felt in Athens. We feel that the cultural differences; the powerful, sometimes ancient traditions; and the sheer numbers of people are tremendous obstacles to the gospel. And so they are. But there is no wall too thick for the power of Christ to topple. As Corrie ten Boom learned from her sister, "there is no pit so deep that God's love is not deeper still."[1] Moses wondered how the Pharaoh could possibly take Him seriously, but God promised to be with him, to empower him. Joshua wondered how he could possibly follow an act like Moses, so God told him, "Be strong and courageous" (Joshua 1:6–7). He would be with Joshua, and He would empower him. Jeremiah said, "Oh no, Lord GOD! Look, I don't know how to speak, since I am [only] a youth" (Jeremiah 1:6). God told him never to say that, never to be afraid of anyone, for the Lord God would be there to deliver him.

Every man or woman who has ever served God has been plagued by self-doubt. God says, "It's not about who you are— it's about who I am. Just look, and see what I see; then speak, and say what I tell you."

Deeper into the City

But what can we do? Paul's brand of boldness helps, but we need a strategy too. Paul and his partners, Barnabas, Silas, and the others, always had a detailed plan before they left for a mission trip. The Spirit of God revealed the destination, but they didn't go without a strategy.

Ray Bakke is an urban prophet of today and chancellor of Bakke Graduate University, which develops Christ-centered leaders who work within business and culture to change cities. One of his books is called *A Theology as Big as the City*. His message is that, as we go into the city, we can't simply see ourselves as pastors to the faithful; we must be chaplains to the whole community. He says:

> The deeper I go into the city of Chicago where I've lived and
> served, the more clearly I see the blood lines of our people

traced back to Poland, to Ireland, to Korea, to El Salvador, to Mississippi, to West Africa . . . the whole city, not my people or my neighborhood alone, is to be the focus of ministry.[2]

He is seeing beyond the outer skin, seeing people in three dimensions with distinct histories and characteristics. Bakke wants us to know who people really are—then, seeing them, have compassion as Jesus does. So the first part of the strategy is to understand people's context.

This isn't the same as a marketing strategy. There has been a certain conventional wisdom that "birds of a feather flock together" and that we should therefore try to reach one demographic at a time. In other words, reach people who walk and talk and look like we do, and our churches will grow more quickly. The problem is that this mind-set sees people as demographic profiles rather than who they are truly are. Bakke is critical of the homogeneous approach. We are the church, and we speak the language of spiritual hunger, not marketing dynamics. We build on kingdom principles, not Madison Avenue concepts. So we must feel God's call to the city, not just to our comfortable, suburban neighborhoods.

During my journey, I began to think about the "birds of a feather" strategy in light of our country's lostness. I asked myself, *Is this the best way?* I began to ask others, "Why don't we approach our own country the way we would any other on this planet?" Ours, too, is a lost nation. We have more unsaved people than most other countries.

Bakke began to see his city of Chicago from the vantage point of the Great Commission, a "corner of the earth" where the gospel must penetrate. I began to do the same, looking at my whole region instead of just one community and one demographic group. I began to see people as lost and found. My job is not to choose one kind of people to reach; it is to have a sense of urgency about reaching everyone because every soul is precious to God, and so many are lost.

At our church, our staff began to strategize about reaching Northwest Arkansas. They heard a difference in the content of what I was telling them. Not only had they never heard such things from me—they had never heard such things at all. I'll tell you what I told them: my chosen strategy to reach people, in all their diversity, for Christ. My plan is built around identifying three highly significant factors.

Three Checkpoints

Paul offers us a model. In Acts 17, he insists on seeing the Greeks as lost, regardless of other facts. But he also sees them as a unique people group with their own perspective, and he has a strategy for approaching them based on that perspective. In the same way, we need to identify (1) people groups, (2) cultural clusters, and (3) community distinctives.

People Groups

Careful research helps us identify the various people groups in our city. Then we can build relationships through our better understanding of people. I decided this was our best approach for our part of Arkansas, as we laid out before our churches a vision about reaching people. This meant I needed to find someone who could help me understand how many people groups live in Northwest Arkansas. We began to seek out specialists to help us do that. After exhaustive research, we learned that in our region of just under four hundred thousand people, we had a total of sixty-five distinct people groups. The largest group, of course, is the great cluster of Caucasians, including its many subcultures. Other groups are rather large; many are not. Some are identified with specific geographical areas; others are more widespread.

We learned all kinds of new things we might have lived and died without knowing, never having been able to serve Christ through that knowledge. For example, the largest gathering of the Marshallese people, outside of their native Marshall Islands in the Pacific, is located right here in Northwest Arkansas. Learning that, we were energized by an opportunity we didn't even know God had placed before us. For the very first time, I looked at Northwest Arkansas as I would look at a country across the ocean. What is the difference, really? Countries "over there" have many people groups; "over here" is the same. In either case, we need to build bridges to those groups, attempt to win people in them to Christ, and through them launch healthy, multiplying churches.

Once our task force understood we were talking about sixty-five varieties of mission, we knew we couldn't do it alone. This in itself is a breakthrough. What we could do was approach our extensive network of small groups and ask them to adopt identifiable people groups. Each would have one group to learn about, meet, serve, and love. Bridges would be built. Even if one group can only do so much for a given people group, this is a start. It transforms people in Bible study groups into Great Commission specialists, missionaries in their own land.

It's exciting to follow the progress of such a radical new idea, our church strategically mobilizing through our membership to reach the specific area of Northwest Arkansas. Once we identified the Marshallese people, our church immediately began to build a bridge of friendship to them. We began a Bible study specifically geared to that group and saw people start coming to Christ immediately. Before long, we found ourselves planting a church among the Marshallese in Northwest Arkansas. Cross Church Marshallese became the first Marshallese Southern Baptist church in all of North America.

God is moving. Miracles are taking place. Most Christians want to see miracles; they simply don't realize that these become commonplace when we step out onto the front lines for Jesus, giving ourselves to Great Commission work. If our eyes hadn't been opened, we'd never even have known about the Marshallese people in our midst. Now, some of them are going to heaven with us, and their own story as a church in Northwest Arkansas is only beginning. The best is yet to come.

And the miracles lead to more miracles. As it happened, the JESUS Film Project, which has been shown in so many nations and languages across the world, is being produced in the Marshallese language for the first time.[3] Thank You, God! Now we have an incredible tool for our Marshallese church. Not only that, but we can make a trip to the Marshall Islands to share the gospel using that film. Some of the new believers from our church plant will be traveling to their native country to help win their own people.

Wouldn't you love to be a part of something like that? Believe me, it isn't a Northwest Arkansas thing—it's an everywhere thing. God cooperates with people who are willing to do whatever it takes to fulfill the Great Commission.

Cultural Clusters

Not only do we need to identify the people groups in our communities, but we also need to look for cultural clusters. By this we mean pockets of people who have come together because of the identifying culture they share. For example, we identified a cowboy culture in our region. These people have built a sub-culture based around that distinctive identity. Why not plant a church perfectly suited for cowboys? Why not plant three? That's exactly what we're doing in our region, each with a goal to win and disciple cowboys for Christ.

Less unique, perhaps, is the business culture. This is a culture we had already penetrated, although we hadn't thought of it as a "cultural cluster." We just knew we needed to meet the business community where it was and help people learn to think biblically about workplace issues. In chapter 1 I described the Summit, a luncheon that meets at our Pinnacle Hills campus. It interfaces nicely with our new understanding of people groups and cultural clusters. To this day, we reach mostly folks who are not members of our church. They plug in because we've built credibility, investing ourselves in their lives and concerns.

What kinds of cultural clusters can be found in your community? There are more of them than you might expect. Why not begin studying your area and identifying them?

Community Distinctives

It is essential that we take the time to identify the people groups and cultural clusters in our communities. But there are also distinctives of your community. For example, you might well have a business cluster as we do, but yours would be unique to your area. In our Northwest Arkansas community, in Bentonville and Rogers, we have what is called "Vendor-ville." This is a group of at least twelve hundred vendors of the corporate giant known as Walmart. These vendors are mostly national or international in their reach, and they are here for one purpose—to service their Walmart account. That's a community distinctive of this area. Fayetteville hosts another one: the community that exists around the University of Arkansas. A large university is a kind of city in itself, and a distinct one. Students, faculty, administration, support services, university police, businesses catering to young people—all of these create a distinctive that we call the "University of Arkansas community."

Do you see the advantage in being obedient to the Great Commission when you take time to know the people of an area intimately, to know who they are and what their challenges are? Now when you visit our church, you meet people with a passion for the Marshall Islands; others who want to talk about a revival happening among cowboys; still others asking you if you've heard how God's Spirit is moving in middle management of the business community.

You can see why I came out of my one-year journey with my head spinning. On the one hand, I saw lostness as I'd never seen it before. I grieved over our world and the vast numbers of people who do not know Jesus and who stand in danger of passing from this earth without having their sins forgiven. On the other hand, I saw the Great Commission as I had never seen it before—paths for God's Spirit I had never known about. For me, someone who had almost always been passionate about the Great Commission, this was a dramatic breakthrough.

It's exciting! The challenge has never been more imposing, but the opportunities have never been greater. It's not your grandfather's Great Commission, perhaps, but I believe it's your heavenly Father's.

Two Keys

Let me also suggest two keys to hold in mind as you plan to capture your community for Christ:

Customize

I hope this book is an encouragement and a resource, but

what worked in one part of Arkansas will differ from what works for you.

As churches, we are prone to imitating one another. This program or this approach worked for church X, so fifty other churches try it the next week. It's a positive thing that we're listening, helping each other, and always looking to serve Christ more effectively. But imitation is a symptom of a plain vanilla ministry instead of a dynamic ministry that meets people where they are and ministers to their needs. The gospel is the same: one Lord, one faith, one baptism. We never change the message, but we change the language with which we share it.

Christ comes to each of us as individuals. He doesn't minister generically, but almost genetically. Study the miracles and healings of Jesus, and you'll find they had a different process with each individual, based on that individual's need. In the same way, we must know the DNA of our community. It's time to do our homework, learn what makes a community tick, and devise a plan based on what we've learned.

A nice benefit is that you'll fall in love with your community all over again as you get to know it better. That's what God does for people who are willing to serve Him. We see needs in high-def clarity, our hearts take hold of us, and nothing is going to stop us from meeting those needs through the power of Christ. The more we know about the Marshallese people, the more we love them; and it's happening with every other group, cluster, and every distinctive area we reach. Paul wrote,

I have become all things to all people, so that I may by all means save some. (1 Corinthians 9:22)

That's Great Commission thinking.

Be Deliberate

This means being conscious of our actions, intentional about what we do. We are never passive; always on the attack. We are careful to be flexible in our planning, and we make room for the Holy Spirit to act. But we don't sit around and wait until we feel supernatural leading either. The Great Commission is always God's will. That's a given. If we know people who are without Christ, we don't need to pray about whether to reach out to them. We know what God wants, so we plan deliberately. Then we are asking on a daily basis, "What are we doing to reach that group this week? How is this part of our plan going? How could it be better?" We have to work to keep our feeling of urgency, to remember that time may be very short. So we have to use that time as wisely and effectively as possible. We have to act deliberately and proactively.

It's hard work. People will not get involved in the strategy unless I succeed in laying out the vision to them and in letting the Spirit implant Great Commission hearts within them. The mission mind-set is a work of constant sacrifice. It requires our time and our treasure, and of course it includes moments of discouragement, even heartbreak. But wasn't it like that for Jesus? Didn't Paul shiver in a Roman prison, feeling at times as if he'd been forsaken by his friends?

We won't give in, even if we face serious roadblocks. We will learn to be tough, as good missionaries do. When we resist the devil, he flees every time. When a new outreach initiative doesn't quite succeed, our disappointment will be counterbalanced by a miracle in some other corner. Besides, we don't always see the end result of the seeds we plant. Only in heaven will we know the impact we've had. So we give it our greatest effort. We do the homework, learn the territory, customize the plan, act deliberately at all times, and pray hard for an amazing harvest. Glory to God in the highest! Bring it on.

Talking Points

I realized after my year of transformation that I wanted to be able to describe our vision clearly and simply and to help our people do the same. I could imagine someone asking a member of our church, "What's up with Cross Church and this community thing? What's that all about?" I didn't want to think about folks getting confused looks on their faces and replying, "Well, it's complicated. I'm not sure I can put it into words." Nor did I want to imagine positive yet vague answers such as, "Well, we're just really fired up about the Great Commission. You know, missions and witnessing and all that." I wanted every one of our members to be able to articulate the vision. The question was, how would we boil this new movement down to essentials so that we could capture it powerfully and specifically in a few sentences?

We reflected, prayed, and discussed this over a period of time because we felt it was important. We're not where we should be as an evangelistic church, even though we've been considered strong in that area for many years. I'm sure most pastors will tell you they'd like to see vast improvements in the effectiveness of their church's evangelism. So we saw this as our opportunity to really "nail" the ideas that were becoming so important to us.

In a few short months, our team formulated the following three-prong evangelism strategy to reach our community.

Personal Equipping

Ephesians 4:12 speaks of equipping the saints for the work of ministry. We can't send people out to share their faith without good training for the task. They need the confidence that comes from understanding what is involved in a good presentation of the gospel. It was time to find the right resources—curricula, instructors, training times—to equip our people to share Jesus.

Because this was so vitally important, we made it the highest priority in our busy church's work. We established tools for deeper evangelism for those specialists who wanted something more comprehensive, as well as more basic tools for the general church population. Our vision was a church filled with people eager and well prepared to share their faith in Jesus Christ, in their own style and based on their personal gifts and friends. We're serious about it, and we still have a lot to do.

Community Engagement

We believe we must engage our community with compassion and the gospel. We look for any opening for serving our community, but we are always centered on Christ and the gospel. In other words, there may be a need for food, clothing, or shelter, and we will meet those physical needs. In each case, we speak the name of Jesus and let His love come through us, so there is the proper balance between physical and spiritual ministry.

People groups, cultural clusters, and community distinctives, of course, play a central role in the way we engage the community. They are the vessels for discovering specific needs that can be met.

Multisite Ministry

We began in Springdale, and a decade ago we planted a second campus in Pinnacle Hills. Now we are located in Fayetteville as well. Cross Church is a multisite church, doing whatever we can wherever we can to reach every person in Northwest

Arkansas with the gospel of Jesus Christ. By constantly planting new churches, we can be much more effective in the areas we want to reach; and with God's help and by His power, we will see this done.

This is what it means to be the people of God. When Jesus left the earth a few weeks after His resurrection, He gave one simple command. We must conclude that it was the most important message He had to leave with us because He saved it for that final moment. He knew these would be the words that those present would remember best.

Jesus wants us to reach every person in this world. The Father doesn't desire that anyone should perish. We love Him, and we know all that He has done for us, so how can we do anything but obey? That's why I'm excited about our new strategy for fulfilling the Great Commission in Northwest Arkansas. It's a plan, but it's not Scripture. We have chosen not to set it in stone, but to travel light with it, growing and changing the plan as we grow and change. Ten years from now, our initiatives may look radically different than they do at present. Visions are powerful and sturdy, but strategies should be light and flexible. Meanwhile, the Great Commission, the gospel, and the need of human souls for forgiveness and salvation will remain just what they are, just what they've always been. And the march toward fulfillment of the Son of God's final earthly request will approach completion. Here's one thing that absolutely will not change: whatever it takes, we will do it! We will follow the wind of the Spirit's momentum and see where it blows.

The Prayer That Lasted a Century

In the early eighteenth century, there was a great German missionary denomination known as the Moravians. You may not know their name, but their fruit lay all across the world. They were way ahead of the curve in the mission movement, simply because they were obedient in prayer and carried out what God told them.

In 1722, their leader, Count Nikolaus von Zinzendorf, established a safe haven for persecuted believers, called Herrnhut ("On the Lord's Watch"). Herrnhut became an incredible community of encouragement and fellowship. Five years later, it sparked a prayer chain.

Have you ever taken part in a twenty-four-hour prayer chain? It's a great experience, but the Moravians kept one active for a *century*. Yes, twenty-four men and twenty-four women made a commitment to pray for one hour of each day, meaning that at any moment, one man and one woman were in earnest prayer. Soon, others were asking if they could take part, and they did. Time passed, and not a moment of it without someone talking to God. The intercessors were organized about it, meeting weekly to encourage one another, follow the progress of their requests, and pencil in new items to pray about. Decades went by, and the Moravians were still on their knees. Children took for granted the ongoing, nonstop prayer as they grew into adults.

As the Moravians listened to God, they found their hearts turning to what matters to Him, and they were planning missions to faraway places. During the first six months, as a matter of fact, Zinzendorf developed a burden for reaching the West Indies, Greenland, Turkey, and Lapland. He told his people about it. The next day, twenty-six volunteers were getting ready for voyages. They understood not just about prayer, but about the importance of acting now. When the first two missionaries were commissioned at a special church service, one hundred hymns were sung. The Moravians did nothing halfway.

Twenty-two missionaries died, and two were imprisoned during the first two years alone; but other believers immediately rose up to take their places. From one little retreat called Herrnhut, with a population of only six hundred, seventy missionaries shared the gospel in other countries—this in an age when no one else anywhere was going on mission trips. There's never again been anything like it in history. My prayer is that churches all across our country will measure up to and even exceed the challenge of those beautiful German Christians.

Everyone who has studied the history of missions knows that the "Father of Modern Missions" is William Carey. Yet by the time he set out to share the gospel, three hundred Moravian missionaries had already been hard at work carrying out the Great Commission.

One more note about the Moravians: a group of them were on a ship that was being tossed about by a terrible storm. Death seemed near, and a young passenger, a struggling missionary himself, was completely undone by terror. Yet he saw these people on the ship singing and praying, completely confident in their God. The young man, whose name was John Wesley, had never seen such powerful faith, such peace in the eye of a hurricane. The experience led him to a divine encounter that made him one of the great men of church history. He and his brother Charles founded the Methodist Church. As I've said, the fruit of the Moravian service is all over the world, including a share in the work of Methodists over the years.

It all began with a prayer chain—with committed, persevering prayer; with listening prayer; with obedience in prayer.[4] So will we pray for God to shake our lives? Will we pray for Him to shake our churches? Will we pray for Him to shake the world?

CHAPTER 6

Talk Jesus Daily

It was one of those defining moments—the kind you won't recognize until months or years later. He was one face in the large crowd of a conference at our church. But every face is one God loves, one for whom He has made wonderful plans since the foundation of time. And in this case, He definitely had something special cooking.

The young man attended our conference and came away elated, simply bursting with excitement and fresh vision. Then he heard that we were looking for a children's pastor, and he realized this was his dream job. He promptly wrote us an enthusiastic letter, detailing the gifts and qualities he could add to our staff team. The young man had everything but the proper qualifications. This was a key staff position that, for a large church, would nearly always require church leadership experience. Our enthusiastic friend didn't have that, and though we loved his passion, we had to file away his letter.

Several months later, however, we again sat and stared at

the stacks of résumés in front of us. There were plenty of good people, experienced and fruitful ministers, none of whom we felt God's leadership to hire. Frankly, we were a bit puzzled that we were finding it so hard to fill the position.

One day my personal assistant walked into my office and said, "Pastor, I think you should revisit one of the past applicants. He never made the short list due to his lack of experience. That's understandable. But as I was going over some of the files, I reread his letter. His words seemed to jump out at me this time. I feel a strong conviction that, at the very least, we should hear him out." My assistant was known for good judgment. I reviewed the letter and agreed to set up an interview, which went exceptionally well. And before long, Dale Hudson, the conference attendee, was our newest staff member.

Dale had the kind of qualities that made us forget standard credentials: a terrific work ethic, a passionate heart for reaching children and their families with the gospel, and the "big picture" of the eternal goals we have in our ministries. As a matter of fact, there are times and situations when it can actually be an asset to lack training. Many fields are changing so rapidly that it's better not to be steeped in yesterday's techniques. Dale knew all about what Jesus called "fresh wineskins" (Luke 5:38). Children's ministry is one of those fields that has changed a great deal during my lifetime, driven by wonderful creativity. Dale was just the man God had prepared to help us minister to families with young children. Our ministry began to grow under his leadership.

One day Dale walked into my office with an eye-opening proposal. He wanted to transform some of our present space into something newer and more contemporary for children. He sold me quickly. I could see how, if we carried out his vision, we'd have one of the most irresistible and effective children's ministries anywhere.

He planned on pursuing a national search to find the one designer in all of America that God wanted for our children's space. I told him to have at it. Dale searched across the Internet, made phone calls, and eventually presented the name of a man he felt understood his vision. "Pastor Floyd," Dale said, "you need to know this man isn't a born-again Christian. And he's never designed a church. But he understands children and the creative use of space. I believe this is God's man to help us reach unchurched families." I understood his point, and I appreciated his thinking outside the box. If we hired someone who specialized in ordinary church work, we would get ordinary church thinking. We didn't want to reach "ordinary church people" though—we wanted to reach the ones who haven't been reached, who stand in need of Christ.

Dale had found a fresh thinker like himself. This man had worked for Nickelodeon Studios and for the interior designers of the Rain Forest Cafés—an innovative, colorful place for families to shop and eat. It's filled with animatronic animals—the kind of thing you would expect at Disney World—and kids love it. He had designed the famous tree at the FAO Schwartz toy store, and even a colorful and animated hair salon for kids. "Fly him in," I told Dale. "Let's hear what he has to say."

It was a fateful day in 1997 when Dale ushered a man named Bruce Barry into my office. Bruce didn't exactly blend into a conservative setting like ours. He had long hair, wore an earring, and dressed in jeans. He also had a smile and personality that brought a room to life in the same ways that his design ideas did. I was amused, and a little intrigued, to hear what he said: "I have no idea why I'm here, Pastor. I've never done this kind of job, and Dale says there's very little money in the budget for the kind of thing that is my expertise. Yet I'm here. Can't tell you why, but I felt a strong urge to get on the plane and do this interview."

Divine Design

As you've guessed, Bruce's interior design was just one element of God's eternal design. After spending some time with the designer, Dale and I knew we were going to do what it took to hire him. Soon he was under contract, the money was being raised, and we were starting to feel the adrenaline. We were going to have the first children's church in America of its bright, colorful kind. We had the vision of a church experience for children that would excite them as much as going to a theme park, all the while effectively teaching them the values of God's kingdom.

As Bruce was building the children's space, we were building a relationship with Bruce. Not that this was any sacrifice, because he was simply fun to be around. As a matter of fact, I wish most Christians I knew had the joy and childlike spirit Bruce brought to his daily life. Yet he didn't know the ultimate joy, the real purpose of a childlike spirit. He didn't know the One who is the source of all his delightful creativity. We really wanted to take Bruce Barry to heaven with us. We found ourselves praying that he would invite Jesus into his heart. The goal was to find just the right opportunity to share the plan of salvation with Bruce before he left town. It helped that Bruce was naturally curious about everything. He had never spent much time around a church or around church people. Now he had the chance to see what people who loved Christ were like. He was moved by the way everyone treated him—the warmth, the courtesy, and the openness of our members and staff.

As his work neared completion, Dale arranged a special luncheon. Its purpose was to give Bruce an opportunity to make some business contacts among our laypeople. I've mentioned that we have some major businesses in our area. Dale, Bruce, and I attended the meeting with a number of business leaders.

It was a nice luncheon, but as we were finishing our food and the plates were being removed, suddenly some kind of cloud came across Bruce's countenance. Something weighed on his mind, and he began telling us about a difficult situation within his family. For some reason, he was choosing this opportunity to open his private world to us. Tears filled his eyes.

I felt that little nudge of the Holy Spirit signaling an opportunity for ministry. I knew that God was ready to do something, though this wasn't exactly the timing I had anticipated. It was a crowded room, filled with high-level professionals. I had shared the plan of salvation many times, but almost inevitably I had done so in small settings: either one-on-one, or with one or two others present. Maybe it seemed counterintuitive to me, but I had learned long ago that God always knows best.

I got up and took a seat much closer to Bruce, so we could make eye contact. I listened to the sadness he had to relate; then I began talking quietly with him about the gospel. I explained the hope it carries, the meaning of being forgiven, and the miracles God can do in the toughest situations. I told Bruce that he, too, needed to become a follower of Jesus. I imagine there were a few eyebrows raised across the room, as many men could hear our conversation.

The agenda for that luncheon had been a presentation by Bruce, not one to him. But that was only a human agenda. Bruce's spirit had been primed by the hand of a wise and loving God. A few minutes later, we were on our knees, with Bruce repenting before Christ, asking for forgiveness, acknowledging a new Lord and Master, and establishing heaven as his eternal destination.

Everyone in the room was deeply moved to be part of such a God moment. Bruce was laughing and praising God, knowing that at that very moment, he had become a new creature in Christ. I helped him set off on the road of discipleship by talking with him afterward about the experience, suggesting his next steps, including baptism and the importance of connecting with a strong, Bible-based church near his home. Everyone left with the jubilation of a mountaintop high. We had come to talk business and design, and we had talked Jesus instead. And, as always in God's scheme of things, other miracles began to take place.

The Chain Reaction

The next day, Bruce came into the offices with a huge smile on his face. He said, "Pastor, I did what you told me. I called my wife last night and told her you saved me. She was so moved by what I told her, she wanted to fly up this weekend so that you could save her too. Could you do that—I mean, could you save her too?"

I smiled, wrapped my arm around his shoulders, and said, "Bruce, I can't save anybody. I didn't save you—it was Jesus who did that. The good news is that He wants to save your wife, Vivian, just as much as He wanted you."

Bruce felt a little sheepish at having used the wrong terminology, but I reassured him. "Don't sweat the wording," I said. "It's what's in your heart, and Christ lives there now."

That weekend, I met with Bruce and Vivian, and I felt a deep joy as she prayed to receive Christ. The couple sat together in our church service. At the end of the sermon, I extended an invitation for people to come to Christ, and the young couple were the first to hurry down the aisle. You'll never see anyone happier than those two were. I was overjoyed as well, filled with gratitude and praise to see God at work yet again. That night I baptized them, and they returned to Tampa and got involved with a great church.

But this was only the beginning of the story . . .

Churches and their leaders talked among themselves. Word began to circulate about the amazing new children's space over in Springdale, Arkansas, and how families were flocking to bring their children to be a part of it. Bruce's telephone began to ring off the hook (a few phones still had hooks in those days). Bruce, who had never worked with a church before we met him, was soon working *mostly* with churches. There was a waiting list to have him come and transform ministerial spaces, and Bruce was absolutely delighted to be such a young Christian yet be in position to use his gifts to bring children and their parents to Jesus Christ. Now, years later, Bruce has done creative design for many of the great churches in our nation. Think about the hundreds of thousands of young, impressionable minds that have been impacted by Christ because of Bruce's gifts.

Why would I tell this story in such detail, aside from the fact that it's a really happy one? To make the point that God does amazing, far-reaching works when we simply prove obedient enough to speak His name—to talk Jesus as a life priority.

Remember, this story begins with what the world would count as a face in the crowd. Dale was a young man who heard God's voice and obeyed. He knew how difficult it would be to be hired by a large church when he had so little experience. We, in turn, knew we were defying the conventional wisdom by hiring him. If we'd done things the world's way, we would have missed some unforgettable miracles.

Then, of course, we had to talk about Jesus to a nonbeliever, without embarrassment or fear of rejection. An evangelistic scenario isn't about our evaluation of our chance for success. It's about doing what Christ has told us to do, telling everyone about Him, making disciples, baptizing them in the name of the Father, Son, and Holy Spirit. Again, though we prepared Bruce by building a friendship, there was nothing intuitive about presenting the gospel in the time and place where we did. Not many evangelism programs will tell you to pick such a moment. But we had to raise the stakes in talking Jesus in God's time, not our own.

Finally, of course, Bruce had to be responsive to the gospel invitation, to an opportunity with his wife, and finally to God's call to change the direction of his career.

Today we still have a thriving ministry to children across multiple campuses. Bruce is impacting children and families everywhere for Christ, and Dale Hudson has gone on to serve terrific churches in Las Vegas and South Florida. If the three of us got together for a reunion, we would have miracle after miracle to share, all happening since that happy event of 1997. That's a lot of kingdom progress in a lot of places, all through the simple work of talking about Jesus.

Jesus walked up to an ordinary group of fisherman and said, "Follow me, and I will make you fish for people!" (Matthew 4:19). They could have never imagined the extent to which they would spend the rest of their lives doing that, nor could they have envisioned the long-term chain reaction that would be set in motion when they dropped their nets. We never know, and that's why we must be obedient in the moment. The spiritual future of nations could be in the balance of your decision to talk Jesus or not. Who but God can say?

What miracles would be happening in your life, and in this world, if you talked about Jesus every single day?

The Invisible Harvest

From the earliest days of my ministry, I've had a strong sense of my obligation to share Jesus wherever I go, person to person. I did it as a young man with his sights set on a call to the ministry; I still do it whenever and wherever I can.

Nothing in life is more rewarding than having a part in seeing another soul enter God's kingdom, and I've had that joy on a great number of occasions. Bruce's story is a striking one, but we could fill libraries with equally amazing stories. I'm sure that among the other new believers I've known, many have had remarkable new lives and ministries without me ever hearing about them. We plant the seeds, but God brings the harvest, and quite often that harvest is not for us to see on this side of heaven.

As an example, consider a Sunday school teacher named Edward Kimball. In 1858, he walked into a shoe store in Chicago and talked about Jesus to a young shoe clerk who was in the class he taught. The clerk gave his life to Christ and became one of the outstanding evangelists of his generation. His name was Dwight L. Moody, and he had a worldwide impact—including in England, where his preaching lit a fire under a pastor named F. B. Meyer, who eventually brought great fruit himself.

Meyer, in turn, traveled to the United States, visited a college campus, and brought a student named J. Wilbur Chapman to Christ.

Through YMCA work, Chapman hired a baseball star named Billy Sunday to share Christ. Sunday, the best-known evangelist of his day, held a revival in Charlotte, North Carolina. The preaching sparked interest in a group of local men, who hired an evangelist named Mordecai Ham to come talk about Jesus some more. And when Mordecai Ham came, he led a young man named Billy Graham to Christ. I doubt I need to say much about Billy Graham's fruitfulness. This man has done his part in the Great Commission, preaching the gospel to 2.2 billion people.[1]

Now I must ask you, do you think the world considers Edward Kimball to be a very important person in the great scheme of things? Had you ever even heard his name? And yet he was one of God's dominoes falling, one by one. Of course someone had to reach Kimball, too—you could follow those dominoes all the way back to the first century. Would you let the chain reaction, which crossed untold generations until the amazing gospel reached and rescued you, end with you? That's a serious question every Christian should consider.

I have made the wrong decisions at certain moments, shrugging off the promptings I felt. Sometimes my own perceptions or agenda have gotten in the way. I listened to the wrong voice. But what might have happened if I'd decided that the time wasn't right for my friend Bruce, during that luncheon? That was a divine appointment, and what if I hadn't shown up for it? I'd like to think God would have reached Bruce in some other way, but it's not for me to know. I simply praise God for showing up on that day and for the fact that none of us got in the way. And may the Lord forgive my selfish disobedience when I fail in the moment of decision.

We need to engrave upon our brains the words of Paul in his letter to the Romans. He stated it so perfectly and with such urgency:

> For everyone who calls on the name of the Lord will be saved. But how can they call on Him in whom they have not believed? And how can they believe without hearing about Him? And how can they hear without a preacher? (Romans 10:13–14)

Everyone has the promise of salvation—just in calling upon the name of the Lord. This assumes repentance and asking for forgiveness of sins. It is a universal promise, but it carries a universal problem: people must hear the name of Jesus in order to call upon it. In other words, there is something for God to do and something for you and me to do. He does the heavy lifting—as I told Bruce, only the Lord can save. But it is up to us to go, to find the lost, and to speak to them the name of Jesus. It's an enormous privilege as well as a profound responsibility. If our neighbors don't hear, if they never realize what Jesus can do for them, then we bear the responsibility for their souls.

That may sound heavy-handed, like just another preacher guilt trip, but remember we are asked to talk *Jesus* daily. If it were truly up to us to save people, then we would have something to be nervous and frightened about. We are only the messengers, the joy sharers, called to talk about something that it should be perfectly natural, even irresistible, to talk about.

The Newbie Factor

All people may be saved by calling on His name. But they won't call upon it if they don't believe. And they won't believe if they haven't been lovingly persuaded. And how can they be lovingly persuaded if you and I decide we have better things to do than rescue the perishing? This is a very serious indictment on how most of us live our lives, and the realization of it should motivate us to do a better job sharing our faith.

But there are more exciting reasons to be motivated too. One of these you might call the newbie factor. Those who frequent the Internet—and today, that's nearly everyone—know that *newbie* is an Internet word for a rookie, a beginner. Newbies tend to be confused by the rules, need lots of help, and get the terminology wrong. Bruce proved himself a newbie in God's kingdom when he asked me if I could save his wife. We simply had a good laugh about that as I set him straight on how to express that idea.

But here's another truth about newbies: they are the world's greatest evangelists. Once we discover something that excites us—a restaurant, a book, a travel destination—we tell everyone we know. Newbies are natural evangelists. It's the "oldies" who tend to become so immersed in the culture that they become complacent and never share their faith with nonbelievers. Some of them no longer even know lost people. Bruce, on the other hand, took about three or four hours to do it. He told his wife. And it didn't stop there. He was talking Jesus wherever he went. His career, of course, allows him to tell the old, old story in a new and creative way. I'm sure he's led many people to Christ and that now he is a spiritual grandfather and great-grandfather to new believers in far-flung places.

It's a fact that many of us can't remember what it was like to be without Christ. So many of us have grown up in Christian homes and don't know what it's like to be lost. But we need to feel the spiritual urgency of those in need of the gospel. We can't be easy-come, easy-go with people's eternal destinies. New believers get it. The before and after of their spiritual condition is fresh and vivid to them. They know it's the most beautiful, amazing transformation they could ever hope to experience, and nothing could keep them from telling others!

Jesus healed a blind man, and the Pharisees were furious because it didn't happen strictly by their rules. They pointed out everything about Jesus that they could twist into negativity, but the young man said, "One thing I do know: I was blind, and now I can see!" (John 9:25). He was telling everyone he saw, even though it put his family at risk with the establishment.

People understand the difference between darkness and light; how can they keep from talking about it? As the old hymn puts it,

> The peace of Christ makes fresh my heart,
> A fountain ever springing;
> All things are mine since I am His—
> How can I keep from singing?[2]

This is why I share the gospel. I have been transformed, and I want as many people as possible to have that same experience.

If I didn't, what would that say about me? In this dark and sinful world, the best people I know are still sinners. I am one myself. There are problems everywhere, yet there is one absolutely perfect place in my world, and that is the place where Jesus Christ makes His home in my heart.

As I look around and see so much darkness, so many people crying out in pain and despair, I want them to know the Light of the World. And the time-honored, premium way of helping them know that light is to talk *Jesus*. We talk about everything else. We talk about football and we talk about what happened on the celebrity dancing TV show last night. We talk about politics, we talk about weather, and we talk about the economy. Yet Jesus, who has rescued us from eternal suffering, who is purportedly the Lord of our lives—about Him we fall silent. We need to learn how to talk about Jesus in a way that is passionate, attractive, and magnetic to those around us. And every single one of us needs to be in on the conversation.

Changes Must Come

It's time for us to come to a new platform from which to launch the great work of this lifetime—a platform from which God can use us to achieve the goal that matters more to Him than any other, and which therefore should matter most to us. But how do we get there?

People Must Change Their Mind-sets

We need to acknowledge that we have let the Great Commission become a sin of omission. Sin comes not only through words but through silence. And here is the issue: It's not simply that there are people "out there somewhere" who are facing eternal punishment. We actually have friends, family members, and neighbors—faces near and dear—who don't know Jesus. We live in states of denial as if this doesn't matter very much, as if it's not our problem. We relegate Christianity to a "lifestyle decision" rather than a decision of eternal destiny. We know better; we're simply in denial.

The denial needs to end. We need to confess our willful blindness to Christ. Then we need to repent and begin talking about Jesus with joy and hope. To repent doesn't mean to try and do better; it means to recognize and repudiate our position, to call it the sinfulness that it is and to turn 180 degrees to walk in the opposite direction. Every single day we should be rising from our beds and whispering:

> Lord, You have given me the wonderful gift of another day. I give You my life for this new day. Guide my steps to the places where You need me. Guide my lips to speak the words people need to hear. I will be fully open to Your guidance. I will hear Your voice. I am Yours for this day.

Do that and believe me, you'll begin a new adventure. The blessings will begin to flow as God uses you in the lives of others. Burden? Duty? You'll love every minute of it.

Talk about Jesus in a sensitive and respectful way, never being pushy or obnoxious. Be a good friend, earning the right to be heard when your friend has a need. Our God is the Lord of time, and He will bring you to the right moment. Simply listen to Him and be open.

Churches Must Change Their Cultures

The old stereotype of the church as a spiritual country club, a polite and comfy refuge from the world, must be discarded. We are a lighthouse, a rescue mission mobilizing to go out onto the rocks and pull the wounded from the wreckage of a fallen culture.

To begin to make that happen, we have to reinvent church life so it's built around discussion, planning, and execution of faith sharing. We can begin by reflecting in our discussions, our sermons, our small groups, and our programs the central priority of our existence. When someone comes to Christ, we need to make a point of celebrating how it happened and lifting it up as an example and a model. People need to understand that blossoms never come unless seeds are planted and that believers are the ones who must scatter the seeds. My observation is that churches who highlight life change have more life change.

Most churches gain new believers and baptisms only through births among existing members. Others simply hope to pick up a few membership transfers from churches across town or when people move into the neighborhood from elsewhere. For all intents and purposes, their strategy is that they won't impede anyone coming to Christ, and they're open to anyone who wants to come and join them—but they have no plans to go out and make disciples. In these stagnant fellowships, the faces remain the same from one year to the next, with a few new babies, a few marriages, a few funerals. These churches float along in their communities like lifeboats in the waters around the sunken *Titanic*, half-full or less, paddling away as drowning people all around them cry out for rescue.

Some churches build "better mousetraps." They erect more attractive buildings and perhaps very nice fitness centers to draw in the community. They expect to start reaching people for Christ once the local people are on campus. Then their neighbors come, enjoy their workouts, and go back home again. Why shouldn't they? We haven't talked about Jesus to them. We have invited them onto the premises and failed to take the next step. Our exciting children's area would have been useless if we didn't talk about Jesus once the families entered it.

Every church sits in a vast, ripe mission field. Each one is surrounded on every side by people who need Jesus. Very few are the churches whose members open their eyes to see the need, open their ears to hear the cries of pain and despair, and go out to do something about it.

We can wrap the package with all kinds of shiny ribbon, but we'll never win disciples until we talk about Jesus with people. We can spend lots of money, we can build large facilities, we can have training sessions, but we still have to start conversations with lost people and confront eternal issues with them. For this to happen, the churches have to repent of their silence, create cultures of soul-winning, as we once called it, and send out the people to share the faith.

How can we avoid the name of Jesus when only He can forgive sin? Only He can change someone from the inside out. Why can't we do it? Let's take inventory of our resources and see what is lacking:

- *Means*. We have the indwelling Spirit of Christ within us.
- *Message*. We have the Word of God, as sharp as any two-edged sword.
- *Market*. We are surrounded by people who need our message.
- *Method*. We have spiritual gifts that together make us the body of Christ.

We have all that we need, other than the will to be obedient. It's time to repent, change our attitudes, and change the culture of our fellowship.

Nine Actions We Can Take to Talk Jesus Daily

We can reach this world! It can be done. We can reach the nations, but we must do it one soul at a time. Salvation comes to individuals. We can go to a people group, but in the end, we must present the gospel to single souls. This is about billions of personal decisions, but in Christ, all things are possible. We are only responsible for our own obedience and availability. Here are nine action points for learning to talk Jesus so that the world can meet Jesus.

Prioritize

It's not difficult to discover a person's priorities. You can read two books to give you the truth: his checkbook and his datebook. Money and time are the great treasures of this age, and how we spend them tells everything about what matters to us. Where our treasures are, there our hearts will be also (Matthew 6:21; Luke 12:34). Many of us obsess over our careers, yet Jesus taught in Matthew 6 that we should worry about what we're going to eat or wear no more than the birds or the flowers worry. God cares for them; would He care any less for us? Jesus said that if we seek His kingdom and righteousness, all the rest will take care of itself.

In short, He has designed our world so that it works only when we set our priorities according to His design. When we place His kingdom first, everything falls into place. When we seek the salvation of others, suddenly we see our own problems for the size they truly are: not very big.

When was the last time you were involved in service—a homeless shelter, a mission trip, a cleanup project? Remember what a good feeling that was, to do something for God and for others? That good feeling came because God wired you that way. Prioritize reaching people and serving God's kingdom, and your life will be what it was always meant to be. How much of our time and money is devoted to Christ, who gave His all for us? How much is purely selfish? Corrected priorities lead to enhanced joy in life, as well as the knowledge that we're following Christ in obedience.

Pray for Opportunities

Through the years I've had a policy of being open to God's opportunities. For the last two years, however, I've been more aggressive on that policy: I've asked God for opportunities to talk about Jesus to someone every single day. "Lord," I've prayed, "let me share the gospel with someone today. I'm here and ready! Give me the time and the person." As soon as I began to pray those words regularly, my life was different. I had far more chances than ever before to share the glorious gospel of Jesus Christ.

First, I know this is a prayer God will answer every time, because it is the very beat of His heart where we are concerned. If you're a parent, imagine how you feel when your child comes to you and says, "How can I be a better child for you? What can I do for my brother and sister?"

Second, this prayer is a particular eye-opener for me. It focuses my mind every day on the reason I'm here, so that the priority of sharing my faith doesn't get shoved to the back of some closet in my mind, with lesser things taking its place.

Once I've started my day with a prayer for opportunities, I'm aware that somewhere, sometime, God is going to open some door. When we know something is about to happen, we are on alert for it. It's like listening for a car in the driveway when you know a good friend is coming to your home. I know

God is lining up something for me, so my spiritual antenna is up everywhere I go, with every conversation I have. "What about this grocery store cashier, Lord? What about the fellow who works at the gas station? How about that neighbor whose path I cross as I'm out taking a walk?"

The battle for a changed life always begins in the mind. I've reoriented mine toward kingdom service, and I highly recommend it to every believer.

Pray by Name

I keep a prayer list. Call me old-fashioned, but it was good enough for George Müller.

Müller started orphanages for children in England during the 1800s, and he fed and sheltered many thousands of children, financing decades of operation on nothing but prayer for God to meet his needs. He never went out and asked for money; he just lived as a remarkable prayer warrior.

In 1897, one year before his death, he wrote in his prayer journal that he had received tens of thousands of answers to prayer in the same day, or even the same hour, that he had prayed them! And yet, he admitted, "I have been praying for fifty-two years, every day, for two men, sons of a friend of my youth. They are not converted yet, but they will be! How can it be otherwise? There is the unchanging promise of Jehovah, and on that I rest."[3]

One of the two men was converted before Müller died; the other a few years later.[4] Müller prayed and kept praying, even when the answers didn't seem to come readily. The result was fifty-two years of powerful and victorious ministry. Do you care enough about anyone to pray him or her into God's kingdom whether it takes days or decades?

On my own list, I pray for all kinds of people and all kinds of needs. At the top of the list are those who don't know Jesus

Christ. I pray for them every day by name. Sometimes I begin listing people I know, and other times the names simply come to mind as I'm praying. I pray for God to open their hearts so they might feel the weight of their sin and their need for salvation. I pray for God to guide the paths of their lives toward a divine appointment. And I pray for God to place me right there at the point of intersection between that person and eternity.

Intercessory prayer is the flip side of the prayer coin. One side is that we pray for ourselves, that we might have the opportunity. The other is that we pray for specific individuals, that we or some other obedient believer will successfully share the gospel with them.

Like George Müller, I've grown confident in God's answers to prayer, simply by His track record in answering my requests. If you feel uncomfortable with the idea of sharing your faith, my counsel to you is to begin praying every day for every unbeliever you know. You will find the fear melting away, to be replaced by a passion for evangelism.

Prepare Yourself Personally and Practically

The boiler room that powers my life is the time I spend with Jesus in His Word every morning. I simply can't imagine not beginning my day this way. You've probably heard this suggestion before. It may be old and familiar, but that doesn't keep it from being essential. You need a daily appointment with Christ to feed your spirit, just as you need daily meals to feed your body. That time alone with God, with the Scriptures, and with a quiet spirit prepares me for the day as nothing else could. I want to be transformed by the renewing of my mind, which doesn't happen all at once, but bit by bit, day by day, as I grow in His Word to become a little more like Christ than yesterday (Romans 12:2).

Something else happens during this time, too: I prepare myself spiritually. When that God-ordained encounter occurs, I will be at my best. Time after time, I find I have read just the Scripture passage I needed to have brewing in my mind before that experience. I will have prayed, and I'll be stronger and more ready. I'll be prepared for victory.

It's also important to prepare ourselves in matters of practicality. That means equipping ourselves to share the gospel. Again, it's not necessary to have an exhaustive, seminary-level understanding of theology to talk about Jesus. However, we need to know the basics of the gospel story and how to communicate them powerfully and effectively. We need to prepare ourselves by considering the questions people might ask and the objections they might raise.

Can you give a strong testimony? The basics are these: (1) your life before you knew Christ, (2) how you met Christ and began to follow Him, and (3) how your life is different. If you've never given your testimony, begin by writing it down. Practice it with a friend. Make it concise, to the point, and compelling; and ask God's Spirit to use it as His tool.

Prime Your Relationships

The most effective witness comes through a powerful relationship. We need to prime our friends for that moment God has prepared. This was what enabled us to share the gospel with our friend Bruce. We built a great friendship; he knew we truly cared about him as a human being long before we ever talked with him about giving his life to Christ.

Isaiah, the Old Testament prophet, spoke of preparing a way for the Lord in the wilderness, of clearing a straight path (26:7). This was a prophecy of John the Baptist, who primed the people of his time to hear Jesus. To "clear a straight path" is to remove obstacles, to smooth the terrain for efficient travel. We are all John the Baptist, in a manner of speaking. We create a path between Christ and someone who needs Him. We seek to clear away every obstacle that would keep that person from hearing His message. The world, of course, places a great deal of garbage in the pathway. We are the road graders who come ahead to push the other stuff aside so that Christ can travel smoothly to that person's attention.

Needless to say, everything we do and say in the context of a relationship is a reflection on our Lord. You've heard those stories about people who drive inconsiderately, even dangerously, all the while with a bumper sticker that reads, "Honk if you love Jesus." Part of our daily prayers needs to be that we would be led in the paths of righteousness for His name's sake. We can actually create obstacles to the gospel rather than clearing them away, so it's important that we be investing our time in people who need Christ. When we do that, we almost can't help but win disciples. When they know how we care, then they will care what we know.

Present the Gospel

Friendship evangelism is a great idea, except when it's all friendship and no evangelism. There must come a time to present the good news, to present it clearly and well, and to ask our friend to make the most important decision of life.

The thought of doing this, of course, strikes fear into the hearts of most Christians. "Me?" they ask with saucer eyes. "I wouldn't know what to say! I would freeze up." That might be true if we were doing the world's work. In reality, this is a God moment. Anyone who shares the gospel will speak of how easily words come, of how much the Spirit of God guides the conversation. In Acts 1:8, Jesus tells us, "You will receive power when the Holy Spirit has come upon you, and you will be My witnesses." Jesus establishes in Matthew 28:18–20 that all authority in heaven and earth has been given to Him, and that He will be with us always. Have you considered that such power and such authority stand behind you whenever you tell people about Jesus? If you are speaking out of your love for Christ, and if the gospel is the center of your message, you carry that power and authority. God will honor your presentation and embody it as a hand fills a glove. But the world's greatest salesperson will accomplish nothing if he or she doesn't speak in the power and presence of Christ. This individual will be like a ship with no wind in its sails.

That's the essence of what we're doing. It's not your speaking ability that changes people. It's inspired conversation that changes people. We need to share the gospel in the power of the gospel for the sake of the gospel. If we are willing to be available to God, He will provide the power. We can toss seeds, but only God can make a sapling break out of the ground and become a mighty oak. We need to season our conversations by presenting the gospel. Pastors need to build their sermon schedules around the presentation of the gospel—too much preaching today steers clear of the only message that can save souls. Sunday school and Bible study leaders need to present the gospel regularly.

I want my life, from now until the day I die, to be a prolonged presentation of the gospel to the world. If I could simply be an effective billboard pointing people toward heaven, I could ask for nothing more in life.

Provide the Moment for Receiving Christ

Can you imagine inviting friends to dinner, giving them light appetizers, and having an hour or two of conversation as they sniff wonderful aromas from the kitchen—but you never sit them down at the table to dine? Failing to make the invitation is like a joke without a punch line or a mystery novel without a solution. We need to build deliberately toward the moment of clearly asking for a decision. We can feed them nice appetizers and lead a nice conversation—perhaps our friends will smell the wonderful scent of godliness—but we must finally ask, "Would you like to receive Jesus into your heart and know that if you died five minutes from now, you would spend eternity with Him?"

As for church, our sermons and our teaching must come to the point, clearly and plainly and inevitably. Whether there is an old-fashioned altar call or a decision is written on a card or some other medium, there must be that moment when the question is put forth, and there must be opportunity for the answer to be determined.

Position for the Future

An almighty God draws people to Himself; we, His servants, share the message. Still, people may decline the invitation for any number of reasons. We will naturally feel a great sense of disappointment when this happens, but remember Müller, who prayed for the same two men for many years. We have to take God's timetable into account.

When people will not accept the gospel, we need to be careful to respect their desires, as much as we disagree with them. The worst possible strategy would be to press the issue, creating tension and even hostility. Once that happens, we've undermined not only our future efforts, but those of other people. Have you ever met someone who felt bruised by misguided, overly aggressive attempts at conversion? We don't need extra obstacles. Instead, we need to think about positioning ourselves for the future. The seeds have been planted. We can now focus on friendship and wait for God to do something. It may even fall to someone else to effectively usher that person into God's kingdom.

We love people, even when we don't love their decisions. That's how God feels about us, right? When they sense that we accept them unconditionally, they appreciate it, and they'll be open to more conversation in the future.

Place Your Trust in the Lord

Whatever happens, praise God and keep trusting.

Our responsibility stops at obedience. It is our task to provide an effective, Spirit-led presentation of the gospel. Anything beyond that the matter rests between that person and God.

So we, too, must rest. This means persisting in prayer, tapping, if not pounding, on the doors of heaven with our desire to see someone come to the Lord. Remember, this is always the Lord's desire too. As the old hymn "Trust and Obey" says, we trust and obey, for there's no other way. To take matters into our own hands, through manipulation or pressing the issue, would be the wrong course. We can't know what God has in store; perhaps down the road He will be more greatly glorified by the way this person comes to accept the gospel. Perhaps God wants you to learn perseverance in prayer. Rest in the knowledge that everything is in God's hands and that you've been faithful. Then, keep sharing the gospel with everyone who doesn't know Christ. The more time goes on, the greater will be your joy and the more abundant will be the fruit you bear for Him.

It all comes down to such a simple thing: talking Jesus every day, in every way.

CHAPTER 7

Desire It Deeply

et's take a peek into the future through a little parable of what could be.

The Parable of Operation Bob

Bob was the kind of man who slipped into and out of rooms without being noticed. He was a quiet, balding, bespectacled man who usually sat on the back pew at church. He was just another professional bookkeeper who worshipped on Sundays—until one particular morning of one particular autumn of one particular year.

The pastor announced a new sermon series on biblical stewardship, pretending not to hear the muffled groans throughout the room.

That's a shame, thought Bob. *People don't seem to like sermons dealing with finance. Yet that's such an important part of life.*

Bob stood up and cleared his throat; the pastor looked his way in surprise. "Might I offer a word?" asked Bob.

"Um . . . Be my guest," replied the pastor nervously.

"It seems to me," said Bob, "that we're approaching this subject the wrong way. Instead of talking about what we can see to give, we should be talking about what we'd give to see."

The pastor, with knitted brow, said, "Fine, Bob. But could you explain what in the world—"

"'In the world' *is* what," Bob interrupted. "I would like to ask everyone to brainstorm for a moment. What could we do if we came to church one Sunday morning, unlocked the doors, and found that God had dropped a check for eighty-six billion dollars down our steeple?"

One snicker, one snort, and several impatient coughs were emitted from the left aisle. "Let the man speak, Wendell—you, too, Myra June," said the pastor sternly.

Bob continued, "Work with me on this, folks. We have a check for eighty-six billion dollars, and we can use it however we want."

"We could build the most awesome Jesus theme park in the galaxy!" shouted a teenager.

His appalled mother quickly stifled the boy and said, "That would be selfish, Eugene. I think we would want to do something to help people with that money."

Someone else said, "You got that right. We could feed a lot of hungry people. And while they were enjoying their meals and helping us plant vegetable gardens for them so they wouldn't go hungry next month—well, I just bet they would listen to us as we told them about Jesus, the One we were doing it for." There were a lot of oohs and aahs for that comment—even a rare "amen" or two. Such responses were unprecedented for stewardship discussions!

"We could hire doctors, send medicine, dig wells, build schools," said someone else.

"Missionaries!" put in a young lady. "Think of the missionaries! We could send armies of really well-trained ones, who could go over with the resources to help, to heal . . ."

"To feed and to preach!" continued someone else. "Can you imagine the Christian presence we would have just about *everywhere*?"

It was then that people began to clap and call out their own ideas. But Fred, the one with the notable snort, spoke over the rising ovation: "Too bad it's all a pipe dream. I haven't heard about God writing any eighty-six-billion-dollar checks lately. Have you? Matter of fact, last I heard, His policy was for us to pay all the bills."

Fred was a known wet blanket. But he had a point, and the conversation stalled for a moment—until Bob asked, "How much of it *is* your own money, Fred?"

Fred stammered a bit, then fell silent. Bob continued, "Maybe it's just me, but the way *I* read the Bible, it *all* belongs to God. 'Giving' is really 'giving back.'"

A few "yeps" and "he's rights" could be heard. (The pastor had taken a seat by this time, neatly tucking his sermon notes into his Bible.)

"And the way I read some recent statistics," Bob continued, "we could easily give back eighty-six billion dollars. That's where I got the number for that check—in an article on the Internet. Those bucks are in our pockets right now, folks—eighty-six billion is what we'd get with standard, 10 percent giving—tithing—from every church member in the United States of America. And these folks have crunched the numbers and figured out that we could wipe out hunger and most disease with that kind of budget, all while sharing the gospel of Jesus Christ."

There was silence for several moments, while people let the thought percolate inside them.

Finally the pastor said, with a deep sigh, "What I wouldn't give to see that."

Bob said, "Precisely my point! It's not what we ought to give. It's what we *wouldn't* give to see God do such wonders. Thank you."

And with that, Bob sat down to let the service continue.

Only it didn't. It couldn't. Nobody could get the pictures out of their minds: pictures of things—wonderful things—happening because Christians actually obeyed God and honored Him with the first tenth of all God had entrusted to them. A woman who was respected by everyone stood and said, "I think maybe God showed up today. I move that we take ten minutes, or however long it takes, to pray and decide as individuals what we ought to do about this thing."

Ten minutes later, it began: people standing up at their seats to announce that they had never honored God with the first tenth of everything, but now they knew it was time to start. There were a few tears, a few outbreaks of applause and whistles. It was starting to sound like a political rally.

True, a small handful thought the whole thing was crazy and walked out—but they were counteracted by a number of people who were so excited, they committed to give enough extra to make up for those who couldn't or wouldn't give.

The next few weeks, the money began to come in, by hand, by mail, by transfer. Some of them were signed commitments to give, but there were some remarkable "first fruit" gifts too. People sold luxury cars, jewelry, real estate. Two families came forward to say they were going somewhere, wherever needed, to share the gospel themselves. Seven teenagers announced calls to seminary and then missions; several single adults were looking into trips overseas.

The grapevine was rattling with news of that crazy Sunday. People called the pastor, and he simply smiled and referred them to Bob. Soon Bob was telling the story over and over, in front of other churches and ministry organizations whose members sat with their jaws on the floor.

Bob's YouTube testimony went viral. And quite naturally, everyone wanted to get into the act. The idea caught on like rustling wildfire—and right in the middle of an economic recession. People simply called it "fulfilling the Great Commission," but the media, not too clear on biblical terminology, began talking about "Operation Bob." They just about scratched the tops of their heads off, trying to figure out what it was about Bob that could set off such a movement. He only shrugged and said it had absolutely nothing to do with him. Then he asked if they would like a copy of the New Testament.

Estimates were that if Operation Bob had been one organization with a single budget, that budget would have exceeded 100 billion dollars. Even as some refused to give, others gave 30, 40, or 50 percent—and the result was an economic boom as so much capital became liquid.

In a way no one had expected, Americans were exporting goods, labor, and people again—*in the name of Jesus Christ.* Who knew?

It was the most revolutionary event since circa AD 30.

• • •

What would you give—or what *wouldn't* you give—to see the revolution break out across this planet? To see God's church go on the offensive, sharing the gospel with supreme urgency and all-in commitment?

Welcome to my dream.

Can you imagine the chain of events if all the followers of Jesus Christ got serious about underwriting His work? If we came together and began something new, based on the proposition that God owns everything and we should bring in His kingdom by giving back? That would be a nice starting point. And then, as giving began to resemble what it should always have been, what if churches decided to focus their budgets on fulfilling the Great Commission, both in giving and in sending people? It sends a chill up my spine just to think about it.

But this is what I see when I wake up from my visions of the good news and read the real news. I see statements such as this one from a recent issue of *USA Today*:

> "Tithing is in decline," said the Rev. William Hull, a research professor at Samford University and a Baptist minister. "The older generation was taught to tithe. It's not being taught very much anymore."[1]

That's not good news at all.

John and Sylvia Ronsvalle, founders of Empty Tomb, Inc., in Champaign, Illinois, have suggested that eighty-six billion dollars, the number Bob cited in our parable, would be the outcome of every church member increasing his or her giving to 10 percent.[2] That's an *addition* of eighty-six billion dollars—in other words, on top of what we're already giving. So our salaries, our programs, and our church maintenance budgets would not be affected—except in catching the inevitable overflow of God's blessing.

That's what happens when we're obedient to Him. Ripples would spread outward in every direction, as when you toss a pebble into the water. Good things would transpire in economic growth, reduced crime, better physical and mental health, and everywhere else you can imagine. All of this would simply begin to happen because we would be so busy obeying God, and

He would be so busy keeping the promises He has given us in Scripture.

The Ronsvalles have written that with eighty-six billion dollars, we could meet the essential physical needs of people in every Third World nation. We could finance effective solutions for clean water, sanitation, healthy child care, food, education, immunizations, and a serious attack on poverty.[3] And of course, our nets would be overflowing as we became fishers of men and women.

The Big Picture

The Great Commission, you see, is a comprehensive idea. It's not something we do; it's at the heart of everything we do. It's not a task we go over there to do; it's something we do right where God has planted us, beginning with the lost person in closest proximity at any given moment. It's not about spiritual needs alone but about physical needs; not about the soul alone but the whole body. That means ministering to physical, mental, and spiritual needs wherever we find them.

We need to stop compartmentalizing ideas of our faith and start seeing things holistically. You've probably figured out by now that I'm all about the local church, even as I'm all about the Great Commission. There's no dichotomy between those two. I'm frustrated when I hear people say things like, "Going across the ocean somewhere is all fine and good, but we should start with this neighborhood. We have plenty of needs right here!" Jesus didn't use the word *or* in the Great Commission. He spoke of "Jerusalem, in all Judea *and* Samaria, *and* to the ends of the earth" (Acts 1:8; emphasis added). It's not a multiple choice question, but a to-do list.

I believe churches who aren't winning the lost in their own neighborhoods need to repent, even if they're sending plenty of funding overseas for mission work. We don't clean either the interior of the house or the exterior; we do both. You need to vote in local elections and federal elections. You need to love your next-door neighbor and your around-the-world neighbor well enough to lead each of them to Christ.

Our job is here, there, and everywhere. It involves preaching, teaching, and ministering to needs. It is *vast*. It follows that it will be costly, in every sense of that word. But is it even possible, preaching the gospel everywhere? Making disciples of all nations? Of course it is. The numbers at the beginning of this chapter show that it's more than possible. Basic giving, as prescribed by the Bible, would more than get the job done, just as a few loaves and fishes fed five thousand with enough leftovers for tomorrow's lunch.

What those numbers don't even consider, of course, is that the present pool of Christian believers would not account for all the giving that would occur. Why not? Because the people who were reached would begin giving from the heart too. New believers are the best evangelists. New believers offer their time and passion like no one else. When we reach them, we reap the whirlwind of Spirit-filled expression that comes from their joy.

If the existing Christians simply walked the first mile and gave the first tenth, then they would start an outpouring (not simply of money, of course) that would change the world forever and hasten the return of Christ. It would be something like history's Great Awakenings of the last three centuries, but with exponential results.

The potential exists. It has always existed. But it begins with a caring, giving heart. That's why we have come to the difficult point, in these next two chapters, of facing one of the greatest practical problems in this task—giving. But giving isn't the real challenge—wanting it enough is. If you have ten dollars in your wallet, it's no challenge to buy an item that costs ten dollars or less; you need only desire to buy it. We have all the resources at this moment. The problem is not in the wealth, but in the will.

Being a disciple of Jesus Christ means that He owns you, right down to the pocket or purse in which your checkbook resides. He owns your calendar, and He owns your bank account. He owns your relationships, your talents, your work, your opportunities. You are merely a caretaker, a steward of them. In fact, you own nothing, and God owns absolutely everything.

Don't take offense to suddenly learning that you own nothing. It doesn't mean we're penniless peasants who hunker down in the dust outside the palace. No, the doors of the castle have been thrown wide for us. We are the "heirs of the kingdom that He has promised to those who love Him" (James 2:5), not peasants but royalty. He has granted us free access to His throne and all the privileges of royalty. At the same time, it's also true that everything is subject to His Lordship. It's a whole lot better than living in the dust!

To put it simply, *God owns it all*. And that's a point of praise, because only He can rule wisely over the jungle of possessions and finance. It's a deep and rich blessing to turn "our" possessions over to God. If we don't, we won't own them; they will own us. Instead, we lay it all before His throne. Then, in seeking His kingdom above all else, we find that all things are provided for us (Matthew 6:33).

So that's who we are—lost children who were adopted by a King who gave His own Son in order to adopt us into His home. He has given us joy, peace, love, and all that we need, calling us to His embrace as beloved children.

Realizing this, we are speechless with emotion and gratitude. We go before His throne and say, "Father, we are overwhelmed by all that You've done for us! What can we possibly do to serve You? We must return Your love somehow!"

And then a determined look comes across His brilliant, majestic demeanor. His eyes seem to move far into the distance, over the horizon, into lands yet undiscovered. He says, "Go out and bring the others home. My other children. There are so many of them! Go and find your lost, scattered brothers and sisters, wherever they have wandered. Bind up their wounds, give them something to eat, and tell them about Me. Tell them about our kingdom. Bring them home!"

We ask, "But how?"

"I'll give you every single thing you need, and much more. I am giving you kingdom authority and power, so that the gates of hell themselves could not stand against you. Sometimes you'll feel that this is where you're going. But it doesn't matter. This is a battle that has already been won, even though many of My children have not heard about it, or in hearing, they still haven't understood. That's why you must go and bring them home."

That, my friends, is a picture of who we are and what we are about. Why, then, do we believe it is financially impossible? It's not about dollars but desire. Do we want it deeply enough? Do we really have the gratitude to please God in the one thing He wants most?

Let's take a look at our rescue mission from the point of view of resources.

The M Word

As a pastor, I've long known what all Christian leaders know:

1. Money is the subject Jesus raised more than any other.

2. Money is the subject His followers avoid more than any other.

People are tense when the topic is raised. I discovered very early in my ministry that I could speak about nearly anything else from the pulpit, but the second I mentioned finances, the temperature of the room would drop twenty degrees. Church members would rather their pastor stick to the subjects of heaven and hell, although Jesus actually had less to say even about those topics than about how we are to handle our possessions. This phenomenon extends to areas other than the sanctuary. What is it that causes the most discord in marriage? Money. What is everyone fighting about in politics? In business? Money.

For most people in a society, money is the hubcap that turns the wheels of the world. It's how we keep score. The Bible, of course, says differently (which is one reason people would rather we not preach about it); but folks evaluate themselves and one another on the basis of money just the same. Money is power. It's status; it's the skeleton key that (they believe) unlocks every door. So people protect it, plan for it, plot for it, worry over it, covet it, cheat for it, and daydream about it more than anything else.

Many years ago, during my studies, I found myself drawn to the theologies of stewardship, giving, missions, and the Holy Spirit. I spent a great deal of time studying and reflecting upon the issues of rendering to Caesar, Savior, and self. I became very motivated, very driven to communicate what I heard God saying about such a crucial subject.

Jesus said that people's hearts would gravitate to the location of their treasure. If I was going to change people's hearts, I needed to get through that worldly treasure chest that was standing in the way. I wanted people to learn the meaning of the word *stewardship*: the wise and proper management of all that God has entrusted to us, whether it be time, talent, things, or anything else. Our stewardship can never be any greater than our view of God.

As a matter of fact, the connection between the two is tight. It is impossible to be godly and greedy. Those two refuse to coexist—Jesus made the point when He said that we could not serve both God and money. Loving one, He said, will cause us to hate the other (Matthew 6:24). Therefore we must choose. Which master will we follow? Which must we leave behind?

For me, it's a no-brainer; one of those two will love me, bless me, and give me eternal life; the other will do no less than enslave me, leading me on a lifelong chase that never brings satisfaction. Besides, it's not really even a question. Above and beyond my self-concern, the fact is that there is one God. He owns all the wealth and all of anything else. To worship anything or anyone other than almighty God is ultimately an act of irrationality, of logical absurdity.

The biblical approach to life is to acknowledge that we own nothing, and He owns everything. He has entrusted many things to us, and He will hold us accountable for our management of them. How do we make use of this time? How do we make use of this salary? This opportunity? This relationship? This health? All of these are on loan from heaven, and all are given to us for His service. Each one has a gratifying shine when rightly used or is corrupted and corruptive when hijacked.

But what are the heavenly purposes these resources serve? Jesus tells us in Matthew 28:19. He tells us again as we stand before His throne: *Go and make disciples. Make disciples of all the people groups in the world.* So I give money to any cause that will make disciples of all the nations. I use my personal relationships to restore them, and to help others do so. I invest my time in strategies of winning them. I discover how my talents fit into the Great Commission, so that they will contribute to restoring them. I treat my body as God's temple, so that I can be an effective messenger to those children. In other words, I am a servant, a steward. Nothing is my own, though everything He has is available to me. I organize my life around carrying out this two-thousand-year-old mission He has assigned to me and every person I know.

Under New Management

Kevin Miller, an editor and executive at *Christianity Today*, describes the stories he heard as a child from his father. Mr. Miller idolized rich and successful men of business during his time. The stories about these commercial titans all carried messages that, if you had enough money, you would have real power. You could do anything you wanted.

But one day he went to church with his wife and son. Something in the sermon touched his heart in a way he had never anticipated, and he gave his life to Jesus Christ that day. From then on, he was a devoted disciple of His Lord. He read a well-thumbed King James Version Bible and told his son about all the things he was learning. "I've started to tithe, Kevin," he said with a smile. "It's quite an adventure."

When Kevin's father died, there were many people at the funeral. A woman walked up to Kevin and said, "You probably don't know me, but I was once in a terrible, abusive marriage. I had to escape, or I wouldn't be alive. Your father paid for me to go to college and learn to be a dental hygienist. Nobody knew about it, but he paid for the whole thing. Today, I'm happy and peaceful, and it never would have happened if your dad hadn't saved my life."

Kevin looked back at the open coffin and thought about the

day his father began to follow Jesus Christ. What would have happened otherwise? Maybe he would have accumulated a lot of money, trying to become more like his old heroes, the money men. Perhaps he would have pursued power. Now, laid out in this casket, neither money nor power would have done him any good at all. But he had exchanged so much of that money for acts of loving kindness, and those are eternal.[4] They follow us into the next world, where the Lord waits for us and says, "Well done, good and faithful [servant]" (Matthew 25:21, 23).

History and our own experiences are filled with stories of people like Kevin Miller's father, whose values changed because their hearts changed. It's not a matter of a New Year's resolution or a teeth-gritting effort to be more generous; we have to change from the inside out. What goes in the heart will determine what comes from the hand.

There must come a time when we hear a divine whisper, nod our heads, and say, "Yes, Lord—it's all yours. None of it is mine, nor has it ever been. My eyes are only now opening to what has been true from the beginning. I'm a caretaker for the Lord of the universe, not the owner of any large or small estate. I'm richer by far to be Your steward than I would ever be as the wealthiest worldly king. From here on out, You will guide me in the use of all that I have." And when we come to the place where we can say that, we feel His radiant smile. We hear the quiet voice of the Spirit telling us, "Good, my child. Then the adventure begins. You're going to experience more joy and more contentment than you ever thought were possible."

With the concept of *mine* stricken from our thought processes, it feels as if we're looking at the world through a new pair of eyes. We look at a car and no longer see a status symbol, something to make us appear trendy and affluent to our neighbors; we see a vehicle to take us places where God needs us. We no longer look at a house and see a place for luxury and lazy comfort; we see a setting for ministry, a place to enlarge relationships that will serve God. We no longer see money as something to hoard and covet; we see it as seed to be planted for a harvest in the garden of God's kingdom. Time, relationships, opportunities, career paths—all of these take on new and eternal meanings. The smallest things now have value, because they are part of the fabric of God's work; things that once seemed all-important are now mere means toward an all-embracing passion of serving the Lord.

There are also those wonderful things the world never told us about—the joy of giving, for example. The world is always telling us that giving is drudgery, something to avoid. It never tells us that not only is it more blessed to give than to receive, but it's more delightful. The world tells us to "look out for number one," but it never tells us who Number One truly is. It never tells us about the joy of service or the peace of simple contentment. The world parades superficial, illusory pleasures, bright and tempting but ultimately empty. It hides the truth about all the good things. Have you ever turned on your television set and seen a commercial telling you that you didn't need any more products whatsoever, that "godliness with contentment is a great gain" (1 Timothy 6:6)?

The Spirit of Giving

Where does that all-important "want" come from? The final verses of Acts 4 tell us what it was like when the first generation of Christianity discovered the power of the giving heart. They stopped caring so much about stuff and began caring about each other and the world around them. They began sharing their possessions, helping the poor. It is in these verses that we hear for the first time about Barnabas, whose name means "son of encouragement." He is so encouraged that he sells a field that he owns and lays the proceeds at the disciples' feet. I can just hear him saying, "This land was only bringing a harvest of a little grain. I want to see a harvest of eternal souls."

Such a spirit of generous giving is always tied in with the Great Commission—with reaching new people. Luke, who wrote Acts, tells us that the believers were experiencing God in a new way. "And with great power the apostles were giving testimony to the resurrection of the Lord Jesus, and great grace was on all of them" (4:33).

It is the Holy Spirit who opens our hearts and our hands, so that we want to give. But the thing we want most to share is not finance but faith. A field might bring Barnabas a little bread, but that bread would be consumed and gone. The Bread of Life, on the other hand, consumes us. Jesus gives us a joy that cannot be clutched or horded; it must be shared with the whole world. We need a powerful outpouring of the Holy Spirit upon our lives and churches, because without Him, we will never learn these lessons. We can read them in the Bible, we can hear them in our churches, we can urge ourselves to follow them—but without Him, they will never rule our hearts. Jesus said, "When the Spirit of truth comes, He will guide you into all the truth" (John 16:13).

We need that guidance today; it is our last great hope.

In the early 1980s, I began to fit together the puzzle pieces of stewardship, missions, giving, and the person of the Holy Spirit. A conclusion took hold within me, and I've never lost my drive to follow its implications. The conclusion is simply this: God has given us our lives and our churches and our resources as tools to ensure that every person in this world can hear the gospel and become a disciple. That belief has been the compass that has guided my life and ministry for more than three decades.

I have not always followed it perfectly; my feet have wandered from the path here and there, but when I have realized I had gotten off course and taken my sights off the fulfillment of the Great Commission, I have repented, felt the refreshment of God's forgiveness, and resumed the quest with greater resolve. I have returned, after that, to looking at everything through Great Commission eyes, seeing how everything in this world ties in to our purpose of reaching the nations and making disciples. I have listened a little better to the voice of the Holy Spirit and been more careful to appropriate His power for His purposes.

We are citizens of heaven who are here for recruiting purposes. We have only so many years in this world, and we must use that time to be certain that when we depart, we take along as many people as we can. But even as we see things through a heavenly filter, we deal with this-world realities. This is hostile territory. There are many people who will bitterly oppose the purpose we want to serve. Not only that, but to achieve vast goals, we need vast financial resources.

Let's look at two critical realities of real-world challenges.

The Mission Is Expensive

First, we need money, and a great deal of it, to fulfill the Great Commission. There; we've said it! And as Bob observes in this chapter's parable, people really don't want to hear about money when talking about God. They might reasonably ask, "Why not pursue spiritual goals by spiritual means?" "Not by strength or by might, but by My Spirit" (Zechariah 4:6). That's a good verse; so why doesn't God get it all done miraculously? Why do we really need plain human money, when almighty God has the power to do what He wants?

The answer is that He chooses to win His lost children

through His found ones. He is glorified when we go, when we strive, when we bleed and sweat to serve Him. He knows where our treasures too often lie, instead of where they should lie, so He tests us by asking us to lay them before Him on the altar of sacrifice.

We want to say, "Lord, You own all and can accomplish all. Why don't You just do it?"

But He would reply, "Because I want you to experience it with Me. Therefore I've placed it in your hands—that which I own, the power I have—so that you can experience the rich joy of reaching the world." That is our task. We walk by faith, through hardships and trials, and that allows the lost children to accept Him by faith—rather than the spectacle of you or me walking on water.

As parents of our own children, we don't follow them to school and take their tests for them. We know they will grow by going out into the world and facing challenges. Sometimes we even allow them to stumble, knowing that it's necessary if they're ever going to walk in strength. In the same way, God wants us to do the work to bring His children home. He wants us to raise the money and determine the wisest way to use it. He is with us all the way, speaking to us, encouraging us, empowering us. Miracles do happen.

We continue to walk by faith, and that includes learning to have faith in God concerning our finances. Our world is so lost—our towns, our nation, our neighbor nations—that the assignment is almost unthinkable. It's a vast, overwhelming vision that will require vast, overwhelming finance. And we know that if the money is limited, the vision will be too. It will fall short, as it has for too many centuries.

From a financial point of view, we live in a time of great doubt. Our parents survived the Great Depression, and our generation is just beginning to crawl out of the Great Meltdown. New rules are being established as we speak. People look at the world, and especially their wealth, in new ways. No more is a prosperous future something to take for granted. People have had their greatest and most terrifying glimpse of a life without financial security, a life of hard choices. Nest eggs have vanished; retirement plans have gone awry.

In this very climate, we step forward to ask people to be wise stewards of God's resources—we remind them that He has a purpose for everything. As frightening as their financial prospects may be, far more terrifying is the prospect of millions dying without hearing the saving gospel. Therefore, we ask all Christ-followers to honor God with the first tenth of everything they have, as well as exceed this amount sacrificially and generously.

As a pastor, I can understand why many of our Christian leaders are frightened to deliver that message. "Maybe this isn't the right time," they say. "My people are emotionally and financially fatigued after what they've been through. They're starting from the bottom again, rebuilding their children's college funds, their retirement plans. They don't want to hear me ask them to finance the Great Commission." But that's exactly what God is calling us to do. The timing of it, however it may appear, is no more or less than the testing of our faith. Will we be obedient? Will we hold to His vision for what is most important in this life? Or will our vision fail, so that we settle once more for the cheap goals we call visions?

No, we can't sugarcoat it. The Great Commission requires financial sacrifice. It requires extraordinary faith and discipline. We have to want it; we have to want it deeply.

The Mission Is Expansive

Remember what it was like to be a child and think it was taking too long to grow up?

I played football in our front yard. When none of my friends were around, I played it by myself—with the stadium, the fans, the announcers, the bands playing, and the colorful jerseys all on the gridiron of my imagination. I was the entire Dallas Cowboys team. As a quarterback, I would toss the ball into the air; morphing into the wide receiver, I would catch it. I had a perfect record in those imaginary games. I was never once on the losing team.

Sometimes I would sit down after a while, put the football in my lap, and think, *I wish it were true. I wish I could be grown up and really play on television for a big team.* The next morning, I would get out of bed, look in the mirror, and see that I was the same size and weight as at bedtime on the night before. They told me I was growing, but I knew what I saw!

I found that life had no fast-forward button. I would have missed a lot of wonderful childhood and teenage memories if it had. I would have rushed through a lot of months just to get to Christmas morning, year after year—remember how long it took for Christmas to arrive?

But growth is a process. I believe God made it that way because process means change, and change means growth. Everything is a journey from one destination to another. Jesus was always on a road leading to Jerusalem and to a skull-shaped hill and an ugly cross. Paul was on a road to Damascus, and from there to the rest of the Mediterranean world. You and I are walking our own paths—career paths, family paths, aging paths, spiritual growth paths. The journey is expansive.

When I became a Christian, I thought I had reached the end zone, so to speak. I was saved! Touchdown! What more could be said? Well, as I discovered, there was a lot more to be said, a lot more to be lived. Discipleship is a process, and sometimes a painful one. There are bad patches of road in which God seems to have fallen silent. There are tests and trials, mountain peaks and shadowy valleys.

God says to me, "Keep on walking. With every step, you become a little more mature. Faith is all about the journey— leave the destination to Me."

I say, "I want to fulfill the Great Commission, Lord, just as You commanded! I'm impatient to make it happen. That's a good thing, right?"

"It's another journey. Yes, it's not bad to be a little impatient. That's far better than not caring. But here, too, you must keep walking."

Sometimes I make the journey longer than it needs to be. I don't follow the narrow path Jesus set out; I stray. I take the scenic route rather than pressing forward "as the crow flies." It's called sin. In heaven, it will no longer be a problem. For now, we battle it every day—and this is an important part of the journey.

Spiritual growth keeps us on task, of course. If we didn't grow, we would wander so far away that we would forget where we'd ever intended to go. We would volley from one spiritual fad to another, follow every brief and bright light. Spiritual growth balances us, wises us up, and finally makes us walk more briskly. The more time we spend with God, the more we read His Word, the greater our desire is to please Him. We begin to have that desire, the "want to" that is so important. We begin walking because He wants us to and walking where He wants us to; it's a great day when we discover we're walking because it's what we want too.

We find that the road becomes more and more treacherous. The tests, traps, and trials increase. The sky grows dark, and we experience those doubts that the destination is even reachable. Spiritual growth is the inner fuel that persuades us, even in the tough times, to push forward.

Hebrews 11 speaks of the great characters of the Old Testament—Abraham, Jacob, and Moses—who obeyed God without seeing the fulfillment of the coming of Christ, much less the goal of reaching and discipling the world. They kept walking by faith and not by sight.

> These all died in faith without having received the promises, but they saw them from a distance, greeted them, and confessed that they were foreigners and temporary residents on the earth. Now those who say such things make it clear that they are seeking a homeland. If they had been remembering that land they came from, they would have had opportunity to return. But they now aspire to a better land—a heavenly one. Therefore God is not ashamed to be called their God, for He has prepared a city for them. (Hebrews 11:13–16)

In other words, these were people who understood the journey. They saw from a distance that God was doing something extraordinary, and they obeyed, even though it wouldn't come to fruition in their lifetime on earth. "God is not ashamed to be called their God." I can't imagine a more profound compliment.

I want to see that final goal come to pass. I want to see the Great Commission fulfilled in my lifetime. I want to see the triumphant, glorious return of Christ. I have to want it deeply, more than anything else. I have to want it more than just today's passing spiritual fad. I have to keep wanting it when the church changes the subject, when the world deflects my attention, when the devil raises resistance, when I simply grow older and a little more tired. I have to want it more than anything on earth, short of knowing God Himself. I have to want it in such a way that it's not even about what I get to see—just as it wasn't for Abraham, Moses, or David.

We have to want it. We have to desire it deeply. How deep is your desire to be the kind of person God isn't ashamed to rule? It's our last great hope.

To Capture a City

How do you capture your community when it contains millions of people?

Here is what we've tried in the past: *flee.*

After the Second World War, America saw a phenomenon of middle-class people—churchgoing people—escaping the inner city. It wasn't hard to understand why. Parents wanted safe, wholesome communities for their children, and they headed for the perimeter to build a massive suburban infrastructure. Schools, mall, businesses; everything was in close reach.

The problem was and is that we left a mess behind. The Bible actually says quite a bit about cities and our responsibility to minister there. Churches today need to repent of the sin of abandoning too many of God's people to inner-city desolation.

The good news is that a new breeze seems to be blowing. I can feel it—a new generation of urban disciples ready to follow Jesus into the metropolis.

New York City is but one of the staggering tasks that lie before us. We feel much like the scouts of Moses in Canaan: "There are giants here—we will be quickly crushed" (Numbers 13:28). The needs are as tall the towers, the sin as black as the soot, the numbers mind-numbing.

There was a man named Jeremiah Lanphier who lived in New York City during the 1850s. Those were years of tension, when the shadow of war loomed over America.

There were strikes, depressions, failing banks, long job-less lines, and an air of simmering violence. In this setting, Lanphier accepted a calling as a full-time city evangelist. He walked the streets, knocked on doors, put up posters, and prayed constantly—all to no visible result.

As his discouragement increased, Lanphier looked for some kind of new idea, some possibility for breakthrough. New York was a business town; maybe the men would come to a luncheon. So he nailed up his signs, calling for a noon lunch in the Old Dutch Church on Fulton Street. When the hour came, he sat and waited until finally, a single visitor arrived. Several minutes later, a couple of stragglers peeked through the door. The handful of them had a nice meal.

Lanphier gave his idea another go on the following week. Twenty men attended; at least it was a start. But then forty came on the third week. The men were get-ting to know each other by this time, and one of them suggested he'd be willing to come for food and prayer *every* day. Lanphier thought that was a good sign, and he ramped up his efforts for a daily meal and prayer time.

Before long, the building was overflowing. The luncheon had to move again and again, so high was the demand. The most intriguing element of the "Fulton Street Revival," as they called the phenomenon, was the ripple effect. Offices began closing for prayer at noon. Newspapers were friendly, since there were centralized customers to pursue, and they began to write about the revival. Fulton Street was the talk of the town, with men telegraphing prayer news back and forth between New York City and other cities—yes, other cities had started their own franchises; other godly meet-ings were launching in New York.

The center of the meeting was prayer, and it was okay to come late or leave early, as needed. Hymns were sung in good voice; men stood and shared testimonies. Nor was it a place for the well-known preachers of the day—this was about the working class, businessmen who wanted to share the things of God.

Some historians went so far as to refer to the Fulton Street Revival as the Third Great Awakening, because it lasted for two years and saw as many as one million decisions for Christ. Given the influence of New York City, no one could estimate the national and international impact that spread out from Jeremiah Lanphier's simple lunch breaks. It is well known, however, that great funds were raised for fulfilling the Great Commission. Funny how that idea rises quickly to the surface during every great, historic movement of the Holy Spirit.

Today New York City needs another miracle. It could start on Fulton Street or anywhere else. We don't necessarily need a gimmick or a program. As we cover all in prayer, we know that the best, most permanent way we can reach any city is to identify people groups and start thousands of new churches geared to reach them. It worked for Paul of Antioch, and it still does.

As I've indicated, I believe we're finally awakening to that task. Give us the urban empires, O Lord. Come, Holy Spirit—lead us into the labyrinth, bearing our light. Show us what it takes to capture a city.

CHAPTER 8

Evaluate Everything Financially

William Colgate was ready and restless. He wanted to make his mark in the world. At sixteen, he left home to seek his fortune. He actually carried a bundle of all his possessions over his shoulder. Ambitious young men, with no particular inheritance or prospects on the horizon, started out that way in the early 1800s.

Colgate was British. He knew how to make candles and soap, but neither of these skills suggested any real opportunity. As his tired feet trod toward London, however, he recognized an older man, a friend of the family who had a small canal boat and knew something of the world. When he saw that Colgate was tall on dreams and short on plans, he took the young man aside and said, "I'd like to pray over you, if you would oblige me, and perhaps offer a kindly suggestion."

The two of them knelt and prayed by the side of the road,

the teenager and the older man. William Colgate felt a sense of peace; perhaps he wasn't an aimless wanderer. God might have a plan for him. Then the older man said, "Have you considered the United States? It's a young nation, but it's beginning to thrive—a land of opportunity. Soap may not be such a common commodity there as it is here. Someone in New York could open a factory and get a toehold in the market. Why shouldn't it be you?"

Colgate was taken with the idea. Then the boat captain put a gentle hand on his shoulder and said, "Be a good man, son. Give your heart to Christ and your life to His care. As the Bible teaches us, set aside the first tenth of all that you receive as a gift of thanksgiving to Him. Make a good product, and do so with honesty and an upright life. If you do these things, you can hardly fail to succeed as merchant and man."

Colgate cherished every word of what he knew was powerful advice. He booked passage on a ship and headed for the New World.

The "happily ever after" part didn't begin immediately. Colgate had trouble finding a position when he reached New York City. But he resolved to live by every wise word that had come from the old captain's mouth. If he earned fifty cents over a few days, five cents of it were reserved for God. Then, as he slowly found his way, making a reputation and starting his own business, ten cents on the dollar didn't seem as much of a sacrifice as it had in the old days of scrimping and scrounging. So he tried doubling his gift to 20 percent.

The years passed, and so did the challenge—30 percent.

Still he felt he wasn't giving sacrificially—40 percent.

Why not half and half? He gave 50 percent.

All the while his business continued to prosper. His name began to resonate in the highest circles of New York City's business community. Colgate credited God with every item of good fortune that befell him. In the end, as an aging and wealthy man with a diversifying business portfolio, he was signing over *all* of his income (yes, 100 percent) to the work of God. Why not? The Lord owned it all anyway, and He could do much more with it than Colgate. The aging entrepreneur needed no more material possessions.

The Colgate company (later Colgate-Palmolive) made soap, and then a product with which the name is much more easily associated: toothpaste. His family gave so much, so generously, that in time, Colgate University (first founded as a Baptist seminary) bore the respected name.

Colgate had a tremendous Great Commission spirit. He fully funded one foreign missionary, while giving untold financial gifts to the Baptist Missionary Union so that the gospel could be preached in every country and disciples could be made.[1]

If only we had all received the kind of advice William Colgate did. If only we would put it into practice even now:

- Love and obey the Lord.
- Give back to Him the first tenth of profits.
- Be honest and do good work.

Can it really be that simple? How can such a path really be argued against, when it has so rarely been tried?

Colgate evaluated everything carefully; then he did the honest work and held true to the promise he made to God. As he continued to evaluate his finances, he determined that greater gifts were in order.

We need to want God's kingdom deeply, but desire isn't enough to fulfill the Great Commission. That work takes resources, so we must evaluate everything financially.

Where to Begin

I know many good people, devoted followers of Jesus Christ, who have the best intentions in the world. They want to do the things that please Him. But somehow life gets away from them, and they find it impossible to serve God the way they intended. Why is this?

It's because they haven't evaluated their plans from the outset. It's all too easy for us to float through life, taking things a day at a time, without setting goals and holding ourselves accountable. Sometimes we're the least intentional about that which is most important to us.

For example, chapter 7 explored what might happen if all Christians put their money where their mouths are. We could solve most of the physical problems of the world, which would give us a great boost in attacking the true sin problems of humanity. We could send missionaries everywhere. And as we made new believers, our work would only become more fruitful. We could do that if we were simply committed and intentional in our giving. Here is what happens instead: according to 2009 figures, the average church member gives only 2.56 percent of his or her income to any church or charity.[2] If you've learned anything from this book, you've learned that our task is massive, and that we need to wake up and face reality. We certainly can't accomplish massive goals with such miniscule giving.

I've often said that I'm astounded by the selfishness of God's people. Yet could it be that some of it is simple disorganization? Simple failure to evaluate everything financially, based on the values by which we should be organizing our lives?

There is a way forward, a clear and simple beginning we can make based on positive and obedient action. Let's examine what these actions would be.

Action 1: Give at Least the First Tenth of Your Income to the Local Church

Malachi 3:10 offers God's provision and His promise:

"Bring the full 10 percent into the storehouse so that there may be food in My house. Test me in this way," says the LORD of Hosts. "See if I will not open the floodgates of heaven and pour out a blessing for you without measure."

I'm certain most Christians have heard this verse quoted. But it isn't the first time we see the idea of the tithe in Scripture. In Genesis, Abraham encountered the Lord and gave Him a tenth of all that he had (Genesis 14:20). In the New Testament, Jesus called out the religious leaders for failing in justice, mercy, and faithfulness, and said that these spiritual duties should be attended to without neglecting the tithe (Matthew 23:23). In other words, it's not a matter of service versus giving. *Both* are commanded of us. The Bible, from Old Testament to New, consistently calls upon us to understand two things in this regard: (1) God owns it all, and (2) we are to give the first tenth of everything, as an act of obedience, thanksgiving, and remembrance.

Malachi 3:10 speaks of bringing the first one tenth to the storehouse. That was the temple treasury, and from its proceeds, funding was drawn for the work of the priests and other services. Today, of course, the church fulfills these functions. It is the successor to the temple as God's house, and we bring our tithes here.

For the church as the fellowship gathering of God's people, we still begin with the first tenth. Paul counsels the church at Corinth, "On the first day of the week, each of you is to set something aside and save to the extent that he prospers" (1 Corinthians 16:2).

Note that the first tenth is given on the first day. In this way, we are always living out the reminder that the Lord comes first in all that we do, all that we are.

Yet our studies show that we're giving one-quarter of the bare essential gift. Perhaps that's where God stands in the heart and priority of the average Christian: about one-fourth of one-tenth of a wholehearted commitment to God. When we think about that possibility, no other word but *repent* comes to mind. We must wake up to the reality of where we are, understand how far we've fallen, confess our sins, receive our forgiveness, and begin serving God with all our hearts.

In defense of laypeople, let's acknowledge that we don't hear enough sermons on this topic. Many believers simply don't understand what is expected of them. They haven't received any strong exhortation to give joyfully and sacrificially, nor have they heard inspiring testimonies of how victorious life can be when we give in joyful obedience to God. Pastors, church leaders, evaluate all of your schedules and plans. Will you preach on giving? Will you equip your people through classes and small groups? No one should be afraid of the backlash. Take a close look, and you'll always find that those who complain about stewardship teaching are the same people who are giving little to nothing. Continue not to train them, and they'll continue to live the same way.

We pray for revival, we pray for miracles and for Christ to return, and we pray for many other things. But there is also a time for action, a time to hear God saying, "Why are you asking Me? I've given you your directions. Go and carry those out!" We need to be obedient in giving, because we are quenching the work of God through our small-minded, close-fisted habits of financing His work.

But what about a struggling economy, a high jobless rate?

These things never enter into the question. Obedience is a policy for all seasons.

Richard Wurmbrand wrote a little book called *Tortured for Christ*. It has been read all over the world. In it he says that while in Romanian captivity behind the Iron Curtain, the political prisoners tithed their one slice of bread and a bowl of dirty soup per week. It was all they had, period, and still they applied biblical principles of giving. The prisoners would take the tenth part of their bread and give it to whoever was suffering the most. On the tenth day, Wurmbrand would give his bowl of soup away. If starving men can do that to honor the Lord as they starve in prison, what excuse do you or I really have?[3]

The tithe is not a policy of convenience, or an option to consider, or an exercise for the super-spiritual. It's for everyone, at all times—as is the blessing that comes from offering it. Remember that God's shovel is bigger than yours; you will never outgive Him.

Give Over and Above the First Tenth of Your Income

Now that we've walked the first mile, let's gaze down the road and think about the second. If we walked one mile, we could walk two, right?

God doesn't give conditionally or proportionately to us. His tender mercies are new every morning. They overflow. We couldn't count them all if we spent the rest of our lives checking them off. Occasionally there are wise believers who come to realize that fact—wise believers like Mr. Colgate—and they begin to do a little overflowing themselves. Remember, we are being transformed to the image of Christ rather than conforming to this world. Each day, we should resemble Him a little bit more. If that happens, there's no way we won't begin to resemble His open-hearted generosity.

In 2 Corinthians 9:6, we read about the law of sowing and reaping: give a little, get a little. Invest a good bit, and the return is similar. It would be wonderful if human investments worked this way, wouldn't it? People pour money into the stock market with absolutely no assurance of getting their investments back. Our economy took a terrible blow because of this principle. There are conservative stocks and high-risk stocks, but no ironclad ones. God's economics work a little differently. We reap exactly what we sow.

The world says to save, hoard, and invest with extreme care. The Word of God says to give lavishly, just as we love lavishly. Jesus says, "Give, and it will be given to you; a good measure—pressed down, shaken together, and running over—will be poured into your lap. For with the measure you use, it will be measured back to you" (Luke 6:38).

We give over and above what is expected because we see that God has given over and above to us. Who could have expected Him to offer to us His only begotten Son, knowing what we would do to His Son?

Also, we come to understand how this principle of godly economy works. The more we give, the more blessed life is for us. C. S. Lewis offers these wise words on giving:

> I do not believe one can settle how much we ought to give. I am afraid the only safe rule is to give more than we can spare. In other words, if our expenditure on comforts, luxuries, amusements, etc., is up to the standard common among those with the same income as our own, we are probably giving away too little. If our charities do not at all pinch or hamper us, I should say they are too small. There ought to

be things we should like to do and cannot do because our charitable expenditures excludes them.[4]

In other words, giving ought to be sacrificial. Like the improving runner who discovers a single mile is no longer a sufficient challenge and doesn't even cause him to sweat, the mature believer wants to go the second mile. He wants to feel his gift to God, to know that costly gift is fragrant before the Lord.

Leave a Legacy of at Least One Tenth of Your Estate to Your Local Church

If we can give our lives to Christ, we can give our deaths too.

A few years ago, fifty people, all at least ninety-five years of age, were asked what they would do differently if they had life to live over again. One of their three most frequent answers was, "I would like to do more things that will last beyond my life."[5] That can be arranged, and so easily. It's wonderful to know, in the autumn of our years, we will continue to impact this world. How much wealth could be given to God's purposes if all believers rewrote their wills to reflect this priority? A brief appointment with the attorney, a simple will, and it can be accomplished.

It's no different whether your estate is worth $20,000 or $200,000, $200 million, or even much more than that. The principal is less important than the principle. In the parable of the rich fool (Luke 12:13–21), the man's great concern was to build bigger barns in this life, to eat, drink, and be merry. What if he had given even the slightest thought to the fact that there is a life beyond this one, life eternal, making this one seem like the blink of an eye? In the parable, he set nothing aside for God's work, nor did he make any provision for the thing that happened to him that very night—his death. All the grain in his storehouse eventually rotted, when much of it could have been converted to capital that might have served God's kingdom.

Local churches need financial freedom to be able to do all they should in God's name. Never should the body of Christ have to strain for pennies, when its Lord owns all the galaxies. Churches shouldn't have to use their people's tithes to retire debt, when that money could be at work in missions. We can ensure something better in the future through our wills and legacies.

Of course, there are organizations, endowments, universities, and other establishments that make the same request. Many of them are worthy and commendable. But the local church, the church that is home to your fellowship and worship and ministry, lies on a higher plane than any other visible institution. All the others will pass away. The finest universities, the most respected hospitals, the museums—all of these will be gone someday. But the church is God's kingdom on earth, and it will never die. If I'm trying to decide where to invest my money, I want to invest in the thing that will endure. The church wins out.

We love our children, and we want to provide for them. But what better testimony to leave them than the lesson of giving from beyond the grave? What more profound message can you send than the truth that God's work is the most important thing in your life, as well as in your death? I will say it even more boldly. Your resources have been given to you, and not to your children. God holds you accountable for how you use them.

W. A. Criswell, the longtime pastor of First Baptist Church of Dallas, used to tell a story about a character named John Rascus, who placed three hundred dollars in the collection plate and whispered to it, "I'll see you in heaven."

Those in the adjoining pews smiled knowingly at each other; old John was becoming a little eccentric in his own age.

Everyone knew that he couldn't take it with him. There would be streets of gold in the afterlife, but no bills of green.

As they smirked, the collection plate made its rounds. John Rascus's wadded bills were pulled out and placed into the church treasury. Some of it was used the next morning to pay the electric bill. Another portion of it happened to supply gasoline to the pastor's car. A bit more went to seminary education for students, and a nice chunk of it went overseas for mission needs.

John Rascus, like the fellow in Jesus' parable, died in his sleep one chilly evening. He awoke to find himself standing at the gates of heaven, and a young man with a great smile was coming to greet him. "Thank you, Brother John," said the stranger. "I was cold, lonely, and lost in darkness. I saw the lights of your church, and heard the lovely music of an evening service. I wandered in just for warmth, but what I found was Jesus."

By this time, another stranger had joined them. He said, "I was filling up my car at a gas station; so was your pastor, John. We started a casual conversation across our cars, the talk took a certain direction, and before I knew it, I was on my knees, asking Jesus to come into my heart."

Then there was a whole crowd of people. They came running up, calling out, "Thank you!" all at the same time. John, puzzled, asked them to speak one at a time. It turned out that all of them had heard sermons from people who studied at the seminary supported by John's donation. Coming up behind them were scores of people from all manner of nations, though now, in heaven, there were no language barriers. A great tear slid down John Rascus's cheek as he heard about the missionaries he had helped to sponsor with his three hundred dollars. Those missionaries had told people about the love and forgiveness of Jesus Christ, and those people had told others. John's eyes moved across the assembled throng of people. Never in his wildest dreams could he have imagined so many people touched by his little gift. He only wished he had given even more!

As John Rascus walked through the gate and entered the everlasting joy of his final home, the angels talked among themselves. One of them said, "Oh, how I envy these human beings."

Another asked why, and the angel said, "They know what it is to be lost and to be found; to be stained by sin, then washed in the saving blood of Christ. Not only that, but they can do something we cannot: they can take temporal, fading things of earth and transform them into heavenly treasure. That's something not even we angels can do."[6]

You wouldn't want to lose out on such a magnificent opportunity. You won't see your finances again in heaven, but you will see something far richer—the eternal fruit they have brought to heaven. Evaluate everything financially, including the event of your passing.

Leave a Legacy of at Least 5 Percent of Your Estate to the Great Commission

Here is the opportunity to give "over and above" in death. You can tithe your estate to your local church, then leave an *additional* 5 percent directly to the fulfillment of the Great Commission, through the work of your local church. Confer with your pastor and missions representatives, taking care to specify how your gift should be spent: for missions ministries with sound doctrine, geared to evangelism and disciple making, across the world.

An alternative is to leave that 5 percent directly to a mission board. Consider the International Mission Board, the North American Mission Board, a combination of the two, or even another mission board committed to finishing the task. Ask

God how He would like you to allocate your financial legacy to a Great Commission endeavor throughout the world.

Christian universities and especially theological seminaries are strategic choices. They equip ministers and missionaries to spread the gospel. Be certain you're connected with evangelical institutions committed to the infallible Word of God, who are committed to the Great Commission.

Evaluate Everything

In that poll of senior adults, another of the top three things they would do, if they could do things differently, was to reflect more. The world is simply too fast paced. We don't stop to think, to reflect, to evaluate where we've been and where we're going.[7]

Pray daily. Bury your heart in God's Word. Then think hard about your life, your time, all your resources, and how they are being spent. They are precious and finite—time in particular—and someday we realize that they run out. You need to build a little margin into your life, a little time to slow down and consider.

Evaluate everything related to finances. Evaluate everything pertaining to the Spirit. Evaluate your health, your plans, your dreams.

It's a good idea to push pause as one year ends and another begins, to go off to a quiet place, as we know Jesus did, to reconnect with God and reassess life. If you want to be more intentional about life, you have to be intentional about being intentional. That means setting aside a time to evaluate old goals and set new ones. It could be done at the end of a calendar year or sometime during the summer, when life seems to slow down and take a deep breath.

It's so easy to completely forget what we are doing on this planet and why we're here. I believe, to the bottom of my soul, that we are here to do what Jesus commanded before He left this earth at the ascension. Yet there is so much inertia in my life, so much pulling and tugging at me, that I can easily lose my grip on the thing I care most about. I need to keep evaluating, keep a watch over my spirit. So do you.

Let the World Teach Us

Bill and Melinda Gates, along with Warren Buffet, asked the nation's billionaires to pledge to give at least half of their net worth to charity. Their challenge was to do this during a lifetime, through a legacy, or a combination of both. Immediately, thirty-eight of the four hundred richest people of America stepped forward to commit to that pledge—half their net worth to charity.

It's an impressive objective, and I applaud it. I do have concerns about what happens to such a large fund of money. We've seen in the past that massive rock concerts for world hunger or famine, for example, have raised staggering amounts, then encountered leaky pipelines in getting the actual aid to the needy. A recent influx of billions of dollars, given by a group of billionaires to inner-city schools of America, also had extremely mixed results, according to *Newsweek* magazine.[8] Again, only in God's economy do we truly reap what we sow. We know we won't have mixed results; we'll have miracles.

But it's good to see successful people examining their financial fortunes and looking for ways to invest in the future. This is a high level of vision that Christ-followers should note. It's an area where we can let the world teach us a lesson that we should be the ones teaching. Perhaps there are fewer Christian believers who are worth billions of dollars. But what if the wealthiest one hundred followers of Jesus left half of their net worth to the Great Commission? The devil would have to flee the army we could raise!

Why dismiss such thinking as empty dreams? It could happen. It should happen. We, who have hearts awakened by the

Holy Spirit, who know how to love as only the godly can love, should be the most amazing, inspirational givers in the world. Nonbelievers should look at us and immediately think of words such as *generosity, compassion,* and *love.* I don't know why it isn't happening that way. I only know that in Christ, we can do the impossible. At the very least, let's learn a lesson from the world about expansive, overflowing philanthropy.

Let the Churches Evaluate Themselves

In our churches, we can evaluate everything financially. I suggest four courses of action.

Rule Out Needless Expenditures

I say it's time for churches to sit down and take a long, hard look at where the money is going. Every church is abounding in good works, but most of us are also abounding in questionable uses of time and resources. Before we begin or continue any program, we need to ask the hard questions about exchanging time, energy, and funding for something. Does it advance the gospel of Jesus Christ? If not, why are we doing it?

"Well," someone says, "a venerable saint from our congregation started this tradition, and we're sentimental about it." I understand that. Tradition is important in church. We honor the people who have honored our fellowship. Still, we need to educate our congregations about why we exist. Let's go over the mission statement. Does your church have one? Is it concise and pointed? It should say something about evangelism and disciple making. And every program, every ministry, must be evaluated based on how it bears fruit of the objectives in that mission statement.

Sometimes we have to get out the pruning shears. Jesus

spoke of bearing fruit and how the branches that bore no fruit could be cut down (Luke 13:9). Some people may think that sounds cold and heartless, but they need to take it up with Jesus. He is extremely serious about this matter of fruit bearing. He told parable after parable about accountability, about the investment of time and resources. And He made it very clear what the fruit is supposed to be, and how we are supposed to grow it.

If every church staff sat down tomorrow and exercised discipline over its budget and the use of its time, people, funding, and other resources, we would immediately free up many millions of dollars to do what Christ wants us to do.

At our church, I asked our leaders to study our energy conservation. In our first thirty-one months of seeking to be better stewards of it, through assistance, planning, and diligence, we have saved $750,000 and have used 29 percent less energy. With one adjustment in one area we tend to take for granted—energy expense—we found a way to allocate $750,000 for the work of ministry rather than facility costs.

I promise you, we'll be doing more of this! I get excited just thinking about the extra funding we can find to advance the gospel of Christ. I hope your church is doing the same.

Reduce Debt

Consider the millions of dollars in interest that we, God's people, pay to maintain debt levels in our church annually. There must be a better way for us to be stewards of God's money.

The new economy has been a shrill wake-up call on a dark, stormy morning. It reminds us that debt can mean disaster. We need to pay down our debt and attempt to eliminate it far ahead of schedule. Impressive facilities are built with the best intentions, but we need to be wise and careful in the ways we handle the money God makes available to us. New churches are being planted and campuses opened, without ever making expensive property investments. People are doing creative things to avoid that kind of debt, and they use as much funding as possible for reaching people. If we could eliminate debt, we could free up millions upon millions of dollars to fulfill the Great Commission.

Reallocate Resources

Our church televised its services for twenty years—much of that time internationally. Like most pastors, I saw this as a strategic way to preach the gospel to large numbers of people. But over time, I began to be plagued by doubts. I felt a conviction to count the cost of a broadcast strategy.

The conventional wisdom, of course, was that without television, you preached to a room. With it, your reach could be exponential. We received letters from people around the world reassuring us that God was using our telecasts to minister to them.

There was no question that we were bearing fruit—but that wasn't the question. The question was, were we bearing the most fruit for the dollars spent?

I wrestled with God over this matter. During my one-year journey of being utterly devoted to studying the Great Commission, the wrestling became more intense than ever. I knew I was accountable to God, not just for some fruit but for "much fruit" (John 15:8). In the end, we made the decision to reallocate dollars from national and international television to ministries of the Great Commission that focus on mobilizing more missionaries, equipping next-generation ministers, and advancing the Gospel nationally and internationally. I was certain my good friends in other countries could find wonderful broadcasts of gospel preaching, and that money could be multiplied as a direct missions investment to reaching and discipling nonbelievers.

I told our people that someday, perhaps we would feel led to have a widespread broadcast ministry again. For now, we had to be obedient to what God was telling us to do. You can still find us on TV in our region and across our state. At the same time, the Internet makes it possible for people to worship with us anytime, anywhere, even without a television. So with the paradigm changing, it was time to evaluate everything again.

Interestingly, ministries across America are beginning to pick up our broadcasts and move it into other regions—free of charge. It's always interesting to see how God honors obedience.

Be Future-Minded

The changes the Internet has brought present a good example of the way the future keeps changing what we're doing to reach people. The gospel never changes, but the world and its media do. We need to do a much better job keeping a watchful eye on the cutting edge, anticipating—the best we can—the direction our culture is taking. Freeing up our finances, of course, is the best way to be flexible and ready for change.

Christian leaders need to read more, listen better, and be more conversant with what is happening around them. When we see people use their phones in new ways—something we couldn't have anticipated a decade or two ago—we need to ask, "How can the gospel be transmitted through smart phones?" When tablet computers become all the rage, we need to ask, "What kinds of applications will make the gospel come to life on a portable, colorful technology presentation?"

Some of our church's most creative people are working toward fulfilling the Great Commission all over the world—from their living rooms. They're using the most advanced Web technology to put together amazing, attractive sites that reach into all cultures and tell the story of Jesus.

Evaluate everything, including the changes that each new year brings. Have a future-ready faith.

Streamline the Church

Throughout the Christian world we find wonderful, honorable congregations that have served the kingdom of God for many generations. I hold a deep affection for them in my heart, and I also know that many of these churches need to reboot.

Isn't this simply a matter of being realistic? Life works that way. The interior of our home doesn't look the way it did when we first got married. In time, we've learned how to streamline it to fit our needs as a family. In the business world, nobody is functioning with the corporate flow chart they used in 1990. The companies that survive are the ones that have adapted.

When I was a young man, a sociologist named Alvin Toffler wrote a book called *Future Shock*.[9] Given that it came out in the 1970s, it was highly prophetic. Toffler said that the world and its structures were entering a cycle defined only by change; and that the world we knew would evolve so quickly that each decade would render it unrecognizable from the one before it.

The churches that cross the finish line, that wear the victor's crown when Christ returns, will be the ones that refuse to anoint tradition for tradition's sake. They will have made a discipline of pruning the vines that weren't fruit bearing, cutting away ministries and turfs that don't bring new believers into the kingdom of God.

I'm sure every pastor knows exactly what I'm talking about. "We've had this ministry for years; we spend all autumn preparing for it." That's the problem—all that time and energy in autumn should be spent doing what the King wants us to do.

Churches *must* streamline their structures. There need to be tough, honest, loving meetings among leaders and staff, defining why the church exists and what we can do to help it achieve its purpose and nothing but its purpose. Yes, it's a good way to lose a few friends. It can even be a good way to find ourselves looking for another position. But if that's the case, we might be serving in churches that are too far gone to make the transition.

This is a very serious point, and I hope it won't be glossed over by those who truly love the local church. Sometimes the most loving thing we can do for the one we love is to schedule surgery—painful but needful.

Go for It!

I've mentioned two of the three most popular responses of ninety-five-year-olds when asked what they would do differently if they had life to live all over again. One was to reflect more, and another was to do more things that would live on after they die.

The third was to risk more. There comes a time to stop playing it safe, in life and in ministry. Great things have been accomplished for God when people walked in faith and took risks. Allow me to give an example from my church's experience.

We have a three-year vision called Greater Things. One portion of the vision is to mobilize one thousand people in 2012 in a cross-cultural missions experience outside of our comfortable borders in Northwest Arkansas—somewhere in North America and across the globe. Let that sink in for a moment: one thousand people from one church.

We do mobilize hundreds of people locally on an annual basis, but we've never had more than 240 involved in missions outside of our own area in a single year. There is a church I admire, one of the strongest global missions churches in the world, that has never mobilized more than three hundred people in a single year. We're shooting for one thousand. It's visionary, and it's impossible—unless God does something miraculous.

Jesus made a pretty striking promise. He said that if we abide in Him (caring about the things He cares about), then we can ask anything in His name. This is what we're asking, and we feel certain He wants it too. So we have stuck our necks out there, so to speak. We've risked.

As I prayed along these lines, God showed up one day in our men's conference. God is always with us, of course, but there are times when He does something truly amazing. This was one of those times.

God mobilized, within a given twenty-four-hour period, at least two thousand of our people. This happened without any prompting from me. Two thousand people have surrendered and committed their names to the dotted line, to join us in a cross-cultural missions experience outside of our area, somewhere in North America and around the world. At the same time, there were folks from other churches who wanted a piece of that action. They will send at least 350 people. Only God knows how many people will actually go, but our church and others will mobilize more people than ever before in our history.

Now we're moving toward 2012 with some momentum, after seeing a vision and asking God for something impossible. We're counting on more than two thousand people to go out there in the name of Christ and put a good dent in the Great Commission. And it's only the beginning. After such an event, we won't be the same, our people won't be the same, and the places they've been will be changed forever as well.

Planting New Churches

The most exciting and miraculous result of any investment of church time and resources lies in the planting of new churches. As we've already discovered, we can't meet the needs before us with the apparatus currently in place. We need many thousands of new churches to be planted, and we need them immediately.

One of the many beauties of this endeavor is that it's so very practical. I believe any existing church can be about the business of planting new congregations that will meet in homes, in auditoriums, in theaters, or in school cafeterias. We already see this happening all over our country, and with terrific results in reaching lost people. We need Spirit-filled, committed believers who are ready for the adventure of a lifetime. This is why I'm challenging churches everywhere to stop thinking in the old, insular fashion and to start seeing themselves as cells that reproduce again and again with exponential results. The needs are exponential, and our strategy must be as well. Gospel churches plant gospel churches that will plant more gospel churches.

Ask great things of God. Attempt great things for God. Take a few sanctified risks.

Let the Denominations and Networks Evaluate Themselves

Denominations and networks serve at the will of local churches. As our churches are now beginning to ask the hard financial questions, especially in regard to the Great Commission, our churches are going to expect the same from their denominations or networks.

I want to suggest five financial actions your denomination or network of churches should consider. Consider each one, because I believe that to ignore them today will mean repenting of it tomorrow.

Pursue Great Commission Ministries Exclusively

If a ministry does not help present the gospel of Jesus Christ to every person in the world or result in making disciples of all the nations, eliminate it. Is that simple enough?

Denominations do not have to make choices between good and evil. Their toughest choices are choices between what is good and what is best. We need to stop trying to do it all. We need to streamline our finances toward advancing the gospel. Our churches do not give money to denominations or networks for anything other than Great Commission ministries. We want to see the gospel advanced. We choose to do it with other churches, not to maintain traditionally good ministries but to maximize Great Commission effectiveness globally.

Spend Fewer Dollars on Structure

Churches never allocate their money to denominations and networks to maintain structure. That should tell us that fewer dollars should be spent in that direction. These entities need to hear this call, coming from the churches, unless they want the churches to begin considering them irrelevant, unresponsive— and unworthy of financial support.

Churches themselves are simplifying their structures, streamlining, and responding to a faster-paced, changing world. They look at their affiliate organizations and expect no less. They believe less is more, and in the future they will support a denomination or a network that is not burdened by excessive structure, but one that is fit and efficient.

Integrate Systems and Strategies

All systems and strategies need to be evaluated by denominations, and evaluated regularly. Duplications and triplications must be eliminated. We spend too much time reinventing wheels. The answer is for regional, state, national, and international entities to integrate their systems and strategies. If these are not streamlined, churches will once again count these blessings of the past as irrelevant for today and the future. There's no reason for us to let that happen.

Take time to integrate systems and strategies. Eliminate what is not working. *KISS: Keep It Simple, Stewards!* Integration can help this take place. I hope our denominational and network employees won't fear change, but see it as a stimulus to do new and exciting things, leaving the old wineskins behind.

Focus on Missions

Churches will respond generously when mission boards step up their own commitment to the Great Commission. Even these boards have to earn the respect and dollars of local churches today. Years ago, "the mission tag" was enough; those days, however have passed away. Due to the globalization of our society, denominational mission boards now need to saturate their trustee boards and their employee forces with pastors who come directly from local churches.

The Web has changed the world and localized the globe in all of our lives. We can communicate around the world anytime, anywhere, and with anyone. Therefore, mission boards, step it up! Use technology to simplify your work and maximize dollars. Developing a communications center for the gospel can change your own boards and their relationship with local churches. In fact, it could accelerate the Great Commission dramatically.

Reallocate More Dollars to Mission Boards

When denominations and networks begin to do the things I've outlined above, the cheering will begin. Everyone likes a success story; we crave to operate in an efficient organization rather than a frustrating bureaucracy. People and churches will answer with more resources when they see dollars minimized for structural usage and maximized toward mission boards and missionary mobilization.

We need more missionaries in North America and more missionaries across the globe. We need more money for these missionaries to use for gospel advancement, church planting, and future planning for finishing the task. We need to put out the call to people: surrender your life for going to the world—we're ready to send you!

I am convinced the day of denominations is not over if denominations reallocate more dollars to mission boards. Churches want to support missionaries, plant churches, and advance the gospel globally. The groups that listen to these words will be the groups that prosper in the future. While arrogance will lead denominations to irrelevance, radical change for the Great Commission will chart an exciting future.

Please hear my heart. We must evaluate everything financially so that

- we can do more for the Great Commission as individuals;
- we can do more for the Great Commission as churches; and
- we can do more for the Great Commission as denominations and networks.

Have I suggested anything that can't be done? In Christ, for God's glory, and for the Great Commission that gives Him the most glory of all—is there anything He will not enable us to do? Evaluate that.

CHAPTER 9

Act Now

I asked my friends at the International Mission Board for the best information available about world population and the degree of its lostness. What I received was like strong coffee to the soul—a real wake-up moment.

They sent me a Web-based chart with a "population clock." You've seen those city population signs with numbers slowly but surely climbing. This chart was like that, with numbers getting larger based on an algorithm that combines the present rates of growth. I could see the world population increasing before my eyes—an estimate, but a reliable one. The bottom line: world population was growing by about 3 new human beings per second.

Another line estimated the number of people currently alive who are "hearing, but not believing, the gospel." I saw this figure growing at a rate of roughly 1 person per second. Thus, every minute, 180 people are being born, with 60 of them likely to hear but reject the gospel—according to current trends we hope to reverse.

A third line identifying "people not having an adequate opportunity to hear the gospel" was growing at a rate of 2 people per second—120 new people per minute with no realistic chance to hear the greatest news on earth.

But there was a fourth line: "People hearing and believing the gospel." At first, to my horror, the number seemed to be stuck. *Are all our missionaries asleep?* Then I noticed that about every four seconds, the total would grow by 1. Apparently we could expect 15 new people per minute who might hear and believe the gospel; 15 likely to be born again, 165 likely to die once and forever.

I didn't crunch these numbers—they crunched me. It was difficult to sleep after looking at them. Here was a graphic representation of an exploding population, and it implied a contest: lostness versus salvation. *Lostness is winning*, and building its lead every single second. More than ever, I felt an intense sense of urgency. How can we reverse that trend? We need to stop the bleeding—now!

Then, a few days later, as I was working on this book, I read that the world population had, in fact, passed another benchmark. There are now 7 billion people occupying this planet (again, as a careful estimate). The number had been 6.9 billion when I was watching the population clock. *Seven billion.* As you think about that number, consider the thousands of years we've occupied Planet Earth. Do you know when we passed the 1 billion mark? The experts give an approximate date of 1804—just over two hundred years ago, a blink of God's eye. We doubled that by 1927, doubled it again (to 4 billion) by 1974, and we're currently adding a billion people every twelve years.[1]

One more number for you: eight out of ten of the world's young people live in Africa and Asia.[2] In postindustrial nations, population is fairly stable, but it's still booming in the developing world. Remember, half of the people on this planet are currently accessible to us in our efforts to share Jesus and make disciples of all the nations. These are people who live among people groups with less than 2 percent of their population identified as evangelical Christian. You would be right if you guessed that many of these live in Africa and Asia—just the places with exploding populations.

Lest we think all the work is overseas somewhere, we turn our eyes back to New York City. I was there recently, traveling, speaking, and taking a firsthand look at the city's condition. We need *thousands* of new churches planted in the Big Apple alone. Take care not to think as the world thinks, because then you'll feel despair. You'll say, "Ten thousand churches in New York City—just in one place? And what about the other cities of this nation, equally lost? What about the countryside, still needing Jesus? What about the rest of the world, where another billion souls may be with us in a decade or so—unless Christ returns? At least we'll be home free then."

Wait. Let's back up for a minute. "Unless Christ returns." Let's take a closer look at the meaning of that eventuality.

Shark-Infested Waters

You may point out that the return of Christ will make things better, and of course you're right about that. Jesus will come back—hallelujah! At that moment, everything will be cool. It will be a day at the beach, at the moment the lifeguard steps up, blows his whistle, and instructs everyone to get out of the water. We won't have to worry about this Great Commission business then, will we? We'll just dry off, go to the great cookout in the sky, and turn up the party music.

Let's sharpen that analogy, since it involves the deadly serious plans of God. Swimming metaphor, take two:

The lifeguard steps up, blows his whistle, and everyone who can hear it and understand his instruction—which happens to be, "Sharks in the water! Get out now!"—can run onto the beach and be saved. You and I have been fortunate enough to have learned about the dangerous reality of sharks, so we're out of there quickly. But in this metaphor, a great many swimmers don't get out of the water. Maybe they haven't had that shark lesson. Maybe they don't know that the whistle carries powerful authority. Maybe they don't speak the lifeguard's language. No matter the excuse, they see no good reason to leave the comfortable water.

To keep the metaphor brutally consistent with what it represents, the shark will not just get a swimmer or two. This kind of shark gets *everyone* left in the water. The wages of sin, you see, are death—not for a few, but for all who haven't dealt with their sin problems. Maybe a shark can't be that thorough, but God's judgment can.

What if Jesus came back today? There are various estimates of what percentage of global population would receive eternal punishment. Only God knows the state of anyone's soul. But if the world's people were swimming together at the beach, our most careful and conservative estimates suggest that almost 9 in 10 would be doomed at that very moment. It is estimated that among the 7 billion, there are 770 million evangelical Christians.

Of course we need to define our terms carefully. There are an estimated 2.1 billion people in the world who actually call themselves Christians; the smaller number of 770 million indicates those who would testify they have surrendered their lives to Jesus Christ as Lord, resulting in their lives being changed by the Lord. Again, only God knows the state of anyone's soul.

So, to complete our metaphor, you'd walk barefoot on

the sand and find your towel as you heard the heart-rending screams, some of them from people you were joking and playing with only moments ago.

In that scenario, I would be educating people about sharks. Wouldn't you? I would do everything in my power to warn them. I might shout frantic warnings, even if it seemed rude. I might yank at both of their arms, pulling them along, even if that was not politically correct among other swimmers. I would plead with them—anything to get them onto the sand—because I wouldn't want it on my conscience that I knew the truth that would have saved them, but did nothing about it. That would mean I owned their fate, or at least some fraction of responsibility for it, right? I don't want to stand before God with anyone's blood on my hands.

So are you uncomfortable? Is the shark story morbid? Tasteless? Probably so, and that's fine, too, if this is what it takes to help people understand the dire consequences of God's judgment. Not only are we talking about life-and-death issues; we're talking about *eternal* life-and-death issues. The shark could be inches away. We have one shot to get this right. If someone is saved, he is forever saved. If he stands condemned, he will find no court of appeal.

We must take care not to look at the world through worldly eyes, for then we might surrender to hopelessness. Our beach is crowded with 7 billion swimmers! The task of telling them about Jesus, and making disciples of their nations, is outrageous. Some might insist it was impossible.

But Hudson Taylor, missionary extraordinaire to Inland China, said this: "I have found that there are three stages in every great work of God: first, it is impossible, then it is difficult, then it is done."[3] He's right. We know that there is no word *impossible* in God's kingdom. We know that God wants us to do this particular thing—this Great Commission thing. And we know He doesn't give out assignments that cannot be completed.

What, then remains? Simply to act—and to act *now*.

The Fullness of Time

Because of the God we serve, we can tell everyone in the world about Jesus Christ, and we can make disciples of all the nations. We must. God has given us every assurance that we will receive His authority, His power, and His presence for the task. But we must act now.

There are seasons of time and deadlines of opportunity. When the appointed time passes, the chance is gone. The Bible is filled with stories about missed chances, about windows of opportunity that finally snapped shut. The Old Testament prophets consistently offered a message that went like this: "Act now. It's later than you think. God will not forestall His wrath forever." In fact, God is precise in His scheduling. There is a theme in the New Testament concerning the "fullness" of time. Our human time, second after second, minute after minute, is described by the Greek term *chronos*. But there are divinely ordained moments, when all His workings and ours come into alignment for the now-or-never moment. The Greek word for that is *kairos*. The Bible tells us that "when the fullness of time had come, God sent forth his Son" (Galatians 4:4 ESV). In other words, God had the wheels of history turning in just such an alignment that He would send His Son at the opportune moment.

If you study the amazing period when He sent Jesus to us, you understand the perfection of the plan. The Romans had moved like lightning across the Mediterranean world, and they had created viable roads for the first time. They had established an atmosphere of relative peace and order known as *pax*

Romana, meaning "Roman peace." Historians use this term to refer to the two hundred years of amazing stability from 27 BC to AD 180, when the Romans, having violently annexed so much of their world, held it in a relatively peaceful way. This is the precise period from just before the birth of Christ to the end of Christianity's first generation. The Greeks, meanwhile, had provided a language that everyone could share, and a particularly beautiful and evocative language, at that—perfect for embracing spiritual content. A man like Paul could speak clearly and powerfully to people in every country around him and be understood. He could move from nation to nation without crossing a battlefield, because of Roman orderliness. And he could do so on a brilliant network of roads that made such travel possible for citizens for the first time.

Jesus, as you can see, had come at the *kairos* moment, in the fullness of time, just as Galatians 4:4 tells us. And among His first public statements was this: "The time is fulfilled, and the kingdom of God has come near" (Mark 1:15). He understood God's perfect timing, and He knew it was His task to act now. Before He ascended to heaven, He told the disciples to wait in Jerusalem for the Holy Spirit to be poured out—another *kairos* moment. Then they could move forward to fulfill the Great Commission.

In Ephesians, Paul discusses God's "plan for the fullness of time, to unite all things in him, things in heaven and things on earth" (1:10 ESV). So the culmination of history will come when the time is right. All things in heaven and on earth will be gathered together in Christ. God does nothing randomly. His plans are perfect, and they extend to every part of creation, to every detail of our lives. Time is a line of events with a beginning, an end, and countless *kairos* moments in the interim. Ecclesiastes 3 agrees that there is a time and a season for every purpose under heaven.

The times are becoming full for God's people to tell everyone in the world about Jesus and to make disciples of all the nations. For example, we see the explosion of technological power in the twenty-first century, like the building of the Roman roads in the first century. We see the Holy Spirit on the move in many developing countries, churches growing in far-flung places despite intense persecution, a new generation of students who have a global mind-set and are keen on traveling across the world to share the gospel. Instead of the *pax Romana*, we have the *pax Americana*. Meanwhile, our planet is in crisis. Governments are in turmoil, wars continue to break out, morals and standards in the United States are beginning to resemble the worst of pagan Rome, and people live in fear of terrorists who seek weapons of mass destruction. Place those two groups of trends side by side, and it's obvious that something's got to give. The world's conditions are reaching critical mass as the church begins to awaken and the devil establishes a counteroffensive.

This, my friends, is the fullness of time. Therefore *we must act now*. It's our last great hope. We swim through shark-infested times. But how should we act? All the clues can be found in Acts 4.

Rocking the World

The first four chapters of Acts are a textbook on how to overcome the world. Here we have the birth, infancy, and first steps of the church—and it all starts with people coming prayerfully before God.

The young church is energized by the actions of Peter and John, who bring about a miraculous healing and then face down the religious establishment. It has seemed as if Jesus was truly gone, home with the Father; and the days of miracles and truth have gone with Him. Yes, He told them that His followers would perform even greater miracles, but who could believe that? And now, here are these two courageous disciples, taking up right where Jesus left off, standing firm in announcing the gospel. They are on their way to prayer—don't miss that detail—when they encounter and heal a forty-year-old handicapped man. You can imagine the disgust of the religious leaders: *This again? Haven't we already put this miracle movement down?* They try to arrest, or at least silence Peter and John. But it's a losing battle because Peter and John will not go quietly. These men are bold, transformed by the coming of the Spirit. They aren't afraid of anything or anyone.

Now thousands of people are committing their lives to Christ. It's a phenomenon; the religious establishment recognizes a no-win situation. The leaders throw up their hands in frustration and allow the two disciples to go home. The church has won its first battle in the Christian era.

The believers gather to celebrate, and they are boisterous about it; they worship God extravagantly, a party of praise. They lift up their voices in prayers of gratitude to God, and "when they had prayed," the Bible tells us, "the place where they were assembled was shaken, and they were all filled with the Holy Spirit and began to speak God's message with boldness" (Acts 4:31). The room is rocking—literally. The joint is jumping. The Spirit of God is filling and empowering everyone, and that takes the party to a new level.

What an event in Christian history it was. The followers of Jesus, so recently afraid and powerless without their master, were transformed by God's power and the doing of His will. In that one verse is the blueprint for how Christians can shake their churches and their world. It tells what happens when God's people pray, when they gather, when the Spirit shows up, and when they speak the Word of God with boldness. Observe how these actions and events proceed logically, one from another. It's an agenda for your life, for our life as a church, and for the great plan of God for this world—and it all begins with prayer.

When We Pray

We can't read Acts without noticing the place of prayer in this book. People are always praying, and God is always responding. Peter and John happen to be on their way to a prayer meeting when they encounter and heal a crippled man. Later, as they share the whole story in fellowship, the response of God's people is the right one: to pray. We need to learn the lesson that we should pray not just when we need something, but when we need to say thanks.

Have you ever felt the room rocking when God's people pray as if they mean it? There is polite, political, rhetoric-driven prayer, and then there is the authentic encounter with almighty God. Anyone can tell the difference between the two. We know when people close their eyes and are speaking to their friends instead of their God, offering halfhearted sentiments that bounce off the ceiling rather than raising the roof. Genuine prayer is not controlled by volume, pious phrasing, or length, although people emphasize those superficial elements. Prayer is simply speaking to God from the heart, with faith that He will hear and answer. Every great revival in history has been forged in the prayer of committed, persevering believers. It will be the same way with reaching our world for Christ. Prayer is the spark that sets the world aflame.

When We Gather

The first Christians didn't take little breaks from churchgoing. "They devoted themselves [to meeting]" (Acts 2:46). They had no building, but they "broke bread from house to house" (2:46). Their joy was so infectious, their teaching and testimony so powerful, that they were the hot ticket in town. Jesus had promised to make them fishers of men, but the fish were jumping into the nets. People saw the supernatural joy that Jesus-followers had, and they wanted it too. Have you ever considered that simply gathering, or getting together, carries its own power? There's a good reason for this. Jesus promises that "where two or three are gathered together in My name, I am there among them" (Matthew 18:20). We are His body, and a body must be connected in all its parts. It must be together.

The "two or three" principle works the same way with prayer. You should and must have a personal prayer life, but you should also be praying together with your fellow believers—praying as a church, praying as a Bible study or prayer group, praying as a family, praying as friends. When we agree in prayer, Jesus says, He will answer (Matthew 18:19). The Greek word for "agree," *sumphoneo*, means "to sound together harmoniously." It gives us our word *symphony*. Believers praying together are making music to God's ears. Your church gathering should be such a force in your community—if the church shut its doors and moved away, the community would bitterly mourn its absence. The early church had that quality, and neither Jerusalem nor the Roman Empire itself could withstand its power.

InterVarsity Christian Fellowship has for many years sponsored the Urbana Conference, a worldwide assembly for students who wish to consider giving their adult lives to fulfilling the Great Commission. It happens at Urbana, Illinois. The 2009 conference had sixteen thousand attendees from all around the world. Students heard keynote addresses, sang and worshipped, then adjourned to small groups for prayer and discussion. In one hall there were three groups: one Chinese, one Taiwanese, and one from Hong Kong. Dividing partitions separated them, and the dividers were certainly intentional. These nations had fought among themselves for longer than anyone alive could remember. So they prayed and worshipped in a segregated way, in their own cubicles.

One night, as the Chinese students prayed, a burden came to invite the others to join them. The Taiwanese students opened their wall divider. Soon the Hong Kong delegation was there too. Eighty students had torn down physical and political walls because of the unity in Christ we are supposed to have. As word of this spread, Korean and Japanese students were entering the room and experiencing the joy of coming together. "In Christ, we are all one family," said a leader who echoed the words of Paul.[4] "For He is our peace, who made both groups one and tore down the dividing wall of hostility" (Ephesians 2:14). If it happened in the first century, it can happen today. When we gather and pray in God's name, amazing things happen. I've come to understand that as strategic Great Commission servants, we strategize to reach people groups; but only God can blend all the colors together and create a symphony of praise.

Somebody said that 90 percent of life is showing up. Your church needs to show up in a big way. When you do, the Holy Spirit will be your special guest.

When the Spirit Comes

When the disciples had the room rocking after the great miracle and courageous event featuring Peter and John, we are told that the believers "were all filled with the Holy Spirit." That one simple statement is the entire explanation. How could Peter stand and defy the religious leaders now, preaching a powerful sermon, when he had denied Jesus before the crucifixion? Why were the disciples bold and optimistic now, rather than hiding and trembling in fear? It was all possible because the Spirit had come, just as Jesus had foretold.

Jonathan Edwards, who lived in the 1700s, was one of the greatest preachers and theologians of all time. He saw the authentic movements of the Holy Spirit leading to a Great Awakening across the Christian world. His most famous sermon was called "Sinners in the Hands of an Angry God." It was brilliant for many reasons, one of them being that he creatively put his listeners in the shoes of convicted murderers, standing in the courtroom and hearing the judge pronounce their sentence. In those days, the judge would face a convicted felon and give a short, stern sermon, saying things such as, "You will now go to meet your Maker," and, "May God have mercy upon your soul." Edwards turned this formula upside down, speaking as a pastor in the judge's chair. He described the wrath of God that would face *any* unforgiven sinner—even respectable church members like those in the room! He put his congregation on trial.

Edwards was powerful in his delivery; yet he read from a manuscript, word for word, holding the paper up close to his face. He neither ranted nor pounded the pulpit; he read calmly. He delivered the sermon more than once—with wildly differing results, despite a consistent delivery. In one church, there were screams of agony from many of his listeners who felt awful conviction for their sins; joyful weeping from others, who realized Jesus would forgive them. So great was the tension that people left fingernail marks in the pew rails, marks that could still be seen years later. But in the neighboring county, "Sinners in the Hands of an Angry God" brought no response at all, other than people yawning and checking pocket watches.

Edwards accounted the difference to one factor: the presence of the Holy Spirit with the first congregation, and His absence in the second. He said that the preaching of God's Word is the occasion for an awakening, but the Spirit does the work, and He "blows where He wills." The screams and weeping were passing things, he said, but when the Spirit showed up, people were changed—permanently. Whole towns were transformed. Crime rates went down, and churches overflowed their spaces.[5] Elsewhere people weren't praying, and the Spirit wasn't moving.

You can preach with the power of an angel, build facilities to rival the Taj Mahal, offer programs with the ingenuity of the Epcot Center, and hire the Dream Team of church staff. But if you build without a true anointing of the Holy Spirit, you build in vain. You are simply reconstructing the Tower of Babel, trying to get to heaven from the ground up. We need the Holy Spirit because God's temple must be built from heaven down. We need Him to fall on us, empower us, show us what He wants us to do.

Of course, we know what He wants us to do, broadly speaking. We are to share Jesus with everyone in the world and make disciples of every nation. The Spirit came for the first time at Pentecost, as recorded in Acts 2, and He wasted no time making this point. It was the last thing Jesus said on earth, and the first thing the Spirit said among us. The people were given the languages of the world, symbolic of telling about Jesus in every nation.

We cannot have churches empty of the Holy Spirit. It's like having a power outage in your home—nothing but darkness and coldness. If we are going to shake our churches, and shake this world, we must have the Spirit come in power.

When We Speak the Word Boldly

Finally, we're told that these first Christians, being filled with God's Spirit, spoke His Word courageously. When we keep in step with the Spirit, we are fearless; we live on life's cutting edge.

Earlier, the religious leaders had confronted Peter and John, and the boldness they now saw was shocking:

> When they observed the boldness of Peter and John and realized that they were uneducated and untrained men, they were amazed and knew that they had been with Jesus. And since they saw the man who had been healed standing with them, they had nothing to say in response. (Acts 4:13–14)

Jesus had clearly been schooled in the Hebrew law and could hold His own with them in any debate. The disciples, however, had been a motley collection of fishermen and peasants. How could such men suddenly stand up to the most distinguished, eloquent men in Judea? The religious leaders "knew that they had been with Jesus." Then, seeing a fully healed man, "they had nothing to say."

Would you like to shut the mouths of the critics, the doubters, the anti-Christianity crowd? Speak boldly, powered by God's Spirit. Do great things that can't be explained away. Today's churches are easy to criticize, easy to ridicule, because too many of them are fruitless and fearful. They have meetings, members, programs, and fancy websites. But if there is no Spirit-driven boldness, no dynamic growth, no weekly pattern of people coming to Christ, then the world has no respect for them. People need to look at us and say, "These people have been with Jesus." The impression should be so powerful that they want to be with Jesus too.

Have you taken a step back lately, looked at your life, and asked, "What is there about me that cannot be explained outside of the power and grace of God?" In a recent book, Philip Yancey tells a true story of a mission trip to Afghanistan in the early 1970s. This was pre-Russian occupation and pre–Taliban rule. It was the time when teenage youth choirs would often go on tour, and this one had limited permission to minister to internationals, though Afghans were supposed to keep away.

The leader accepted an invitation to perform in downtown Kabul, but it was against what he felt was his better judgment. He warned the teenagers that if they said certain things, they could find themselves in prison, jeopardizing other Christians in Afghanistan. He gave them carefully worded statements to memorize. "Don't get off the script," he said with emphasis.

One thousand Afghans came to hear the Americans performing. The night was going wonderfully—until a teenager put down his guitar and began to speak from the heart.

"I'd like to tell you about my best friend," he said. "His name is Jesus, and He has made an amazing difference in my life."

The leader nearly fainted. From the side of the stage, he began grimacing and making the throat-slash sign: "No! Cut! Stop talking *now*!"

But the teenager was on a roll. Apparently it was a God thing. He went into a detailed account of what Jesus had done in his life. The leader just sat back with his head in his hands, wondering what kind of mess he would be untangling over the next few days. He looked up in time to see the Afghan minister of cultural affairs making his way to the stage. *Here it comes*, thought the youth leader.

The diplomat said, "We've seen many American young people come through this country. Usually they are long-haired youth who come for the drugs they can find here. We haven't seen young people like these. You speak of the love of God, and my country needs that message. I want our young people here in Afghanistan to experience your message. Can your group extend your tour, to visit every college and faculty, and also speak on Kabul Radio so even more can receive the words you have offered? I can make these things happen."

The leader was in shock. He arranged an extension to everyone's visas and to the tour itself. And he gave the kids another warning: "Don't you change a *word* from what God tells you to say!"

The teenagers gave many more performances; and after each one, the Afghan young people would gather around and ask questions about Jesus, who sounded so different from the Jesus they had encountered in the Qur'an. They had never heard of a personal relationship with God—of being fully forgiven and changed inside through faith.

There had never been anything like this in Afghanistan, and it happened because it was a Great Commission moment, a *kairos* moment, in a place where the Spirit of God was determined to move. If the leaders weren't ready to cooperate with heaven, then the Spirit would find a teenager who would.[6]

The Final Act

Yancey's account isn't unique in the annals of world missions, where miracles happen all the time. When Christians are bold enough and obedient enough to move to the front lines of the battle for the human race, when they pray, when they gather in His name, when they speak the Word of God boldly in the power of the Holy Spirit; then, my friends, there are no boundaries whatsoever, no limits to what can and will happen. Jesus said the gates of hell themselves would not prevail against the resurgent body of Christ (Matthew 16:18). Why should we be afraid of merely human opponents?

A miracle happened for a couple of uneducated fishermen

among the most sophisticated and hostile men in Jerusalem. One happened for a teenage guitarist in the heart of Islamic tension. They will happen anywhere, everywhere, and for anyone who is simply willing to act now.

We've read about the Acts of the Apostles, the first Christians, in this chapter. It's time for the acts of this generation, our last great hope. I believe this is the fullness of time, the *kairos* moment when God will find the ones who are ready and willing to be obedient. For those men and women, doors will open, opportunities will present themselves, and the Holy Spirit will come in great power.

Those believers will rock this world. I want to be among them. Don't you?

Great Commission Tech

Two lessons I'll never forget from this period of my life: Lesson one: God wants *all* people—no matter their names or numbers.

Lesson two: God does incredible things to demonstrate that first point.

I'll give you an example.

In another section, I detailed our discovery of a large group of people from the Marshall Islands living, of all places, in Northwest Arkansas. How does that happen? We haven't quite figured it out, but we established the local Marshallese as a people group we wanted to reach. The identification of the Marshallese people group led to establishing a relationship with them, resulting in our teaching the Bible to them, winning several of them to faith in Jesus, and now planting a church with them. This is a God-sized miracle!

Meanwhile, in Orlando, Florida, where the JESUS Film is translated in new languages all the time, the film finally became available in the Marshallese language—right on time! That film, you may know, has been used all over the world to lead millions of people to Christ.

You can see the beautiful symmetry of our church flying a group of Arkansan Marshallese to their homeland, with a fresh copy of the JESUS Film in their language, to share the gospel. This is God letting us go in style. In the fullness of time, His plan for this seemingly obscure culture of people came to fruition. I believe it's His way of demonstrating how much He loves *everyone*. In His eyes, all the nations count, large or small.

But the JESUS Film brings up another factor: the shrewd leveraging of new technology for an ancient purpose.

Dr. Bill Bright lived in Hollywood in the 1940s. When he became a Christian, his original vision for ministry was a film about the life of Christ, accurate to the Scriptures and with high production values, capable of being translated into every language. As things worked out, it wasn't God's timing for that idea. Instead, Dr. Bright founded Campus Crusade for Christ, which has pursued the goal of sharing Jesus with everyone on earth, and making disciples in every nation, creatively and with excellence for decades.

But the JESUS Film was finally made, in the 1970s, and in time it would become—according to no less than the *New York Times*—the film viewed by more people than any on the face of the earth.[7] As Billy Graham quickly learned how to make use of television for the gospel in the 1950s, radio and film have been used strategically.

Then, in the 1990s, the World Wide Web burst onto the scene. In on the ground floor was a Silicon Valley wizard named Walt Wilson. He was an executive with Apple Computer, Inc. during its pioneering days. A few years ago, he left to start a ministry known as Global Media Outreach, which creates thousands of varieties of websites to help people meet and encounter Jesus, then connect with a local church.

How exactly does that work? Wilson understood that several million times per day, people were accessing the

Internet for information about who Jesus was. So there was a clear need to make sure there was good information about Jesus online, well organized and easily accessible. The "aha" moment came in the realization that there were countless millions of times per day when people consulted the Internet about other problems, problems for which Jesus was also the answer: loneliness; abandonment; divorce; abuse; depression. The list could go almost infinitely.

Wilson's group began creating customized websites to minister to people with needs of all kinds, through volunteers and staff who would respond to "clicks" on the site, asking for more information. Christ would be shared at an appropriate time, decisions would be made, and churches were introduced into the dialogue. Millions of people have been reached, followed up, and discipled to date.

But some would say personal computers are old news, right? The latest in technology is the smartphone and its cousin, the tablet computer.

When I think about the potential for spreading the good news about Jesus Christ through cell phones, I can't help but smile. I remember studying about the time of Martin Luther, the great German reformer who took a dangerous stand for the authority of God's Word. In his time, his own German people could not read the Word of God in their own language. He took it upon himself to translate the Latin Bible, then in use, to German—just as Gutenberg introduced the printing press. In the fullness of time, the gospel was ready to travel again.

Through the little "apps," or downloadable applications that are often available at no charge, people have access to the Bible on their phones in nearly any language, in an immediate way. Of course, we still have the problem that half of the world's people are illiterate. That's where a ministry called Faith Comes by Hearing makes a difference. This group is rushing to get audio recordings of key Scripture passages available in mobile phone apps, so that with a simple click, someone can hear the saving gospel in his or her native language.

So even though many can't read, it's still possible to share God's Word with them through Internet and mobile applications that speak their language. It has been estimated that there are more cell phones in Saudi Arabia than there are people. We can't afford to lose a single opportunity to make the gospel available, in every way, in every place, to every nation.

Meanwhile, missionaries can travel with entire theological libraries in their hands through laptop or tablet computers. An inch or two of electronic storage can hold the content of what would, at one time, have been several rooms filled with shelves. The missionaries can study God's Word as they go about their work, perhaps speaking to a missionary friend on another continent, or receiving encouragement from a prayer partner back home—on phone or computer video.

Paul the apostle once wrote letters to churches, trusting to God that the letters would be recycled—literally carried by hand from town to town—so that their instruction could spread. His technology consisted of the crude writing implements of the day, and his delivery technology wasn't much better, in retrospect. The limitations made no difference in the economy of heaven. Technology captures the human imagination, but God's power makes any other form of ingenuity appear feeble.

Even so, we have these tools. Let us use them wisely. Paul knew how to use whatever God put in his hands to tell the gospel story. He said, "I have become all things to all people, so that I may by all means save some" (1 Corinthians 9:22).

With all the tools available to us today, how are you, your church, your network, and your denomination using them to advance the gospel of Jesus? You and I can talk to people in real time, half a world away. We can write blogs, record videos, and design applications that come down to new wineskins for a gospel that is ever fresh, never old. Sharing the gospel in creative ways, real and relevant for the day in which we live, is essential to fulfilling the Great Commission, which is our last great hope.

Our Last Great Song

You've seen it on YouTube or television: the "flash mob," one of those passing fads of our creative culture.

In some public place—a park or a mall food court—people will be milling around, going about their day. Music is piped in from someone's boom box or a public address speaker. A young person begins, all by himself, to dance to the music. Two or three other people wander up and join him. Others pause to watch what appears to be a spontaneous act of playfulness. Then a small group materializes to dance along, right out of the crowd, and we know something's up. Ultimately a massive group appears from somewhere or other, and we have the flash mob, a public, fully choreographed dance event that no one suspected they would behold.

It happened on October 30, 2010—the day before Halloween— at a Macy's store in downtown Philadelphia. Early Saturday morning shoppers, still wiping the sleep from their eyes, wandered through clothing and furniture and cosmetics sections.

They had no idea a full opera company was in their midst; there were no Viking costumes, no theatrical props, only casually dressed shoppers in the aisles and among the sale tables.

At high noon, the largest pipe organ in the world, the mall's historic Wannamaker organ, began playing the opening measures of the "Hallelujah" chorus from Handel's *Messiah*. People scattered throughout the store suddenly stopped shopping and began to sing, "Hallelujah! Hallelujah!"

Non-opera folks looked up, startled. What was happening on a Saturday morning in a Macy's store?

In glorious harmony, people were singing the text taken from Revelation 19:6:

Then I heard something like the voice of a vast multitude, like the sound of cascading waters, and like the rumbling of loud thunder, saying: Hallelujah—because our Lord God, the Almighty, has begun to reign!

Handel's music is insistent, irresistible. "Our Lord God omnipotent reigneth!" sang the choir. "Hallelujah! Hallelujah!"

The first time it was ever performed, in 1742, King George II felt such profound emotions that he leapt to his feet as the chorus sang. As he stood, of course, the people did the same. And to this day, it is customary to stand as the familiar organ strains sound. There's something in that chorus that compels us to joyful worship, something that opens a brief window into the ecstasy of heaven itself. Almost four hundred years later, the piece touches something in people's souls that makes them weep.

As the opera company sang, a wonderful thing occurred. Ordinary shoppers began to sing along. Complete strangers, bags and boxes in their hands, were singing out together. Suddenly a retail store was transformed to a cathedral. It was the very reverse of the thing that drove Jesus to wrath on the temple steps, when His temple had become a marketplace. Now the tables were turned, so to speak!

"And He shall reign forever and ever," sang the people of Philadelphia. "King of kings, forever and ever! Lord of lords, forever and ever!"[1]

The planners of the "Messiah mob" had called it a "random act of culture." But there was nothing random in their part of it. It took planning, rehearsal, strong voices, and then, most important of all, going into the marketplace so that it could be captured. The response of the shoppers, joining in the song, wasn't truly random, either—not if we think about it. The song is irresistible; it gets beneath the skin and takes the heart captive. Once we hear it sung, we can't help but become a part of it.

This, my friends, is a picture of the task we have before us. If we look at the world through weary, doubting eyes, we see a vast, spiritually slumbering marketplace on the threshold of Halloween. So much evil is in the air, and people are interested in little more than buying, consuming, and entertaining themselves in ways that bring only emptiness.

Yet here we are among them, citizens of heaven in their midst: fellow shoppers, fellow consumers. Why don't we see the possibility? Why don't we find our voices? Why not begin singing out, for all we're worth, of our King of kings, our Lord of lords? Don't we know what would happen if we all sang joyfully in unison?

People would not scowl. They would not put their hands over their ears and hurry away. Have you seen that in a "flash mob" yet? If we all sang together, if we sang in lovely, joyful harmony about the majesty and glory of our King—people would stop all they were doing, forget all they were pursuing, and listen with their whole selves. God, after all, has set eternity in their hearts. There are black, aching voids inside them that only Christ can fill—and something within each person knows it; something within would leap up in exultation hearing the music from another world as deep called to deep.

If the thing that angered Jesus most deeply was to make His house into a marketplace, does it not stand to reason that the thing that most gives Him joy is to make the marketplace into His house? Why don't we put together a "non-random act of Christ" in this world? We need to meet among ourselves and learn to sing in harmony rather than discord. We need to strengthen our voices so that the gospel can shine as an otherworldly jewel through us. Then we need to go into all the world, just as Jesus has called us to do, and sing! Sing for all we're worth!

Let's stop finding new ways to merely argue for the gospel or debate with the atheists. Arguments entrench people; they do nothing more than inspire them to rearrange their prejudices. Debates are too much of us and too little of God.

No, what we need is beautiful, harmonious music, out where the people are. The Spirit of God Himself inhabits our praise. His glorious love for humanity abounds in the music of His people. I'm not speaking, of course, of literal singing, though it is indeed a wonderful tool in the hands of the Holy Spirit. I'm really talking about the joy and emotion and love we show among people as we speak the words of the gospel, the truth about Christ; as we mingle and minister. I'm talking about what would happen if we all worked together, if we acted in powerful, organized harmony to share the love of our Lord and the path to salvation. (The Macy's event was put together by the City Opera of Philadelphia but included singers from twenty-eight other musical organizations. Can God's people work together like this?)

I think it's interesting that Saturday, October 30, the day

of that event, was the eve of the devil's day, but also the eve of Sunday, the day of the resurrection. It depends upon whose calendar controls our minds and hearts, doesn't it? Never has so much darkness loomed in our world—and never has so much potential existed to finally go and reach the world for Christ, to make disciples of every nation. We can do that! We can do that because there are many of us, with many resources and tools. We can do it because it has always been possible, from the very moment Jesus first uttered our marching orders. But most of all, we can succeed because God wills us to succeed, His power undergirds our efforts, His authority stands behind our movements, and His presence accompanies our every step.

We may be preparing for the final, ultimate chorus. I feel the rustling of the King's robes as He stands to hear what will come out of our mouths. Will it be the music of heaven, or the gossip and chatter of the world?

Awakening the Great Commission is our last great hope. Positive and personal response is guaranteed from every tribe and language and people and nation. May we seize this special moment, tune our voices to sing His praise, advance into the fields that are ready for harvest, and expand God's glory globally with a song of victory on our tongues.

Notes

Prologue

1. William Carey to Rev. Mr. Fawcett, Halifax, 5 January 1794, in *The Church* (London: Simpkin, Marshall, and Co., 1844), 1:25.

Chapter 1: Face the Truth About Yourself

1. Jim Collins, *How the Mighty Fall: And Why Some Companies Never Give In* (New York: HarperCollins, 2009), 74.

Chapter 2: Awaken the Church

1. Washington Irving, *Rip Van Winkle and The Legend of Sleepy Hollow* (London: MacMillan and Co., 1893).
2. "Six Megathemes Emerge from Barna Group Research in 2010," *Barna Group*, December 13, 2010, http://www.barna.org /culture-articles/462-six-megathemes-emerge-from-2010.
3. "Now, This Bell Tolling Softly for Another, Says to Me, Thou Must Die," in *The Works of John Donne* (London: John W. Parker, 1839), 3:575.
4. Ronnie Floyd, *The Power of Prayer and Fasting* (Nashville: B&H Books, 2010).
5. Mickey Noah, "Church Envisions 50 New Church Plants," Baptist Press article, June 2, 2011, http://www.bpnews.net/BPnews. asp?ID=35419.
6. 2011 North American Mission Board Ministry Report, at http:// www.namb.net/annualreport/.

Chapter 3: Accept the Urgency

1. See http://www.imb.org.
2. Data as of 01/05/2011 as currently available on www.peoplegroups.org. Accessed June 1, 2011.
3. Ibid.
4. Jim Haney, "Global Lostness," Monthly Report of the International Missions Board, 3/31/11.
5. Ronnie Floyd, "Leading for Global Impact," presentation for New York Metro City Conference, 2011, based on figures provided by International Mission Board.
6. Tom Clegg and Warren Bird, *Lost in America: How You and Your Church Can Impact the World* (Loveland, CO: Group, 2001), 25.
7. Sam Roberts, "Listening to (and Saving) the World's Languages," *New York Times*, April 29, 2010, A1.
8. Thomas L. Friedman, *The World Is Flat: A Brief History of the Twenty-First Century* (New York: Farrar, Straus and Giroux, 2005).

Chapter 4: Transform Our Families

1. Matt Carter, "The Church as the Champion of Social Justice," session 6, Together for Adoption conference, Austin, Texas, October 2, 2010.
2. "The Richt Family's Life-long Commitment," *GameDay*, ESPN, October 25, 2008, available at http://espn.go.com/video /clip?id=3663225.

Chapter 5: Capture Our Communities

1. http://www.corrietenboom.com/history.htm.
2. Ray Bakke, *A Theology as Big as the City* (Downers Grove, IL: IVP Academic, 1997), 81.
3. Robert Boyd, "NWQ Marshallese People Translate Popular Religious Movie," *5News Fort Smith–Fayetteville*, April 8, 2011, available online at http://www.5newsonline.com/news /kfsm-nwa-marshallese-people-translate-popular-religious -movie-20110408,0,7970978.story.
4. J. P. Eckman, *Exploring Church History* (Wheaton, IL: Crossway, 2002), 78.

Chapter 6: Talk Jesus Daily

1. Barry M. Horstman, "Billy Graham: A Man with a Mission Impossible," *Cincinnati Post*, June 27, 2002.
2. Robert Lowry, "My Life Flows On (How Can I Keep from Singing)," lines 13–16.
3. Unknown Christian, *The Kneeling Christian* (Whitefish, MT: Kessinger LLC, 2010), 63.
4. Roger Steer, "Seeking First the Kingdom: The Secret of George Müller's Spiritual Peace," *Discipleship Journal* 31 (January/February 1986).

Chapter 7: Desire It Deeply

1. Greg Garrison, Religion News Service, "Few Churchgoers Tithe, Study Says," *USAToday.com*, June 2, 2008, http://www.usatoday.com/news/religion/2008-05-31-tithing-church_N.htm (accessed May 16, 2011).
2. http://www.emptytomb.org/research.html.
3. Craig L. Blomberg, *Preaching the Parables: From Responsible Interpretation to Powerful Proclaimation* (Grand Rapids, MI: Baker, 2004), 51.
4. Kevin Miller, sermon, "Secrets of Financial Contentment," transcript PT296A, http://www.preachingtoday.com.

Chapter 8: Evaluate Everything Financially

1. Max L. Christensen, *Turning Points: Stories of People Who Made a Difference* (Louisville, KY: Westminster/John Knox Press, 1993), 32–33.
2. Dr. Ronnie W. Floyd, Progress Report of the Great Commission Resurgence Task Force of the Southern Baptist Convention (speech to the Executive Committee, February 22, 2010) http://www.pray4gcr.com/downloads/GCRTF_Progress_Report.pdf.
3. Richard Wurmbrand, *Tortured for Christ*, 30th Anniversary ed. (Bartlesville, OK: Living Sacrifice, 1998), 43.
4. C. S. Lewis, *Mere Christianity* (1952; repr., San Francisco: Harper Collins, 2001), 86.

5. John Maxwell, *Leadership Gold: Lessons I've Learned from a Lifetime of Leading* (Nashville: Thomas Nelson, 2008), 247.

6. W. A. Criswell Foundation, "Treasures in Heaven," 2010, www.wacriswell.org/PrintOutline.cfm/SID/806.cfm.

7. Maxwell, *Leadership Gold*, 247.

8. "Grading the Moneymen," *Newsweek*, May 1, 2011, http://www.newsweek.com/2011/05/01/grading-the-moneymen.html.

9. Alvin Toffler, *Future Shock* (New York: Random House, 1970).

Chapter 9: Act Now

1. Department of Economic and Social Affairs, Population Division, "Population Size and Composition," chap. 7 in *World Population Prospects, the 2000 Revision*, vol. 3, *Analytical Report* (New York: United Nations Publications, 2001), 171.

2. "World Population Projected to Reach 7 Billion in 2011," *CNN Tech*, August 12, 2009, http://articles.cnn.com/2009-08-12/tech /world.population_1_fertility-rates-world-population-data-sheet -population-reference-bureau?_s=PM:TECH.

3. Robert J. Morgan, *On This Day in Christian History: 365 Amazing and Inspiring Stories About Saints, Martyrs, and Heroes* (Nashville: Thomas Nelson, 1997), August 27 entry.

4. Corrie McKee, "Asian Students Tear Down Walls," *Urbana Today*, December 31, 2009, 6.

5. Stephen R. Holmes, "A Mind on Fire," *Christian History* 77 (2003): 13.

6. Philip Yancey, *What Good Is God? In Search of a Faith That Matters* (New York: FaithWords, 2010), 219–22.

7. "Bible Film Is the Most-Watched Movie of All Time," Giles Wilson, *The New York Times*, July 22, 2003, page 1AR.

Epilogue: Our Last Song

1. Peter Mucha, "Macy's 'Flash Opera' Has Web Singing 'Hallelujah,'" *Philadelphia Enquirer*, November 19, 2010, http://www.philly.com/philly/news/breaking/20101119_Macys_Flash _Opera_has_Web_singing_Hallelujah_.html.

About the Author

Dr. Ronnie Floyd, senior pastor of Cross Church in Northwest Arkansas, is the author of twenty books and the featured speaker of *Ronnie Floyd*, a television program available on a CBS affiliate. In 2001, his church became a multicampus ministry with messages broadcast live worldwide via the Internet. His proven leadership as a pastor and evangelical leader in global awakening and the Great Commission serves as the impetus for this book. Floyd and his wife, Jeana, have two sons and five grandchildren. For more resources from Dr. Floyd, visit www.ronniefloyd.com.